A CROSS FOR NAPOLEON:

THE LIFE OF FATHER BRUNO LANTERI (1759-1830)

A CROSS FOR NAPOLEON:

THE LIFE OF
FATHER BRUNO LANTERI
(1759-1830)

by Msgr. Leon Cristiani

translated by Keith Mayes
and Madeleine Soudée

ST. PAUL EDITIONS

IMPRIMATUR:
    Niceae die. 12a. mensis Februarii 1957.
    A. Giraud, Prot. Apost. Vic. Gen.

ISBN 0-8198-1404-0 cloth
       0-8198-1405-9 paper

Printed by the Daughters of St. Paul
50 St. Paul's Ave., Boston, MA 02130

The Daughters of St. Paul are an international congregation of
religious women serving the Church with the communications media.

To
His Eminence
Humberto Cardinal Medeiros
on His Tenth Anniversary as
Archbishop of Boston

CONTENTS

PREFACE

This translation of Msgr. Cristiani's life of Father Lanteri is presented on the occasion of the 150th anniversary of his death (August 5, 1830). We hope that it will bring about a more widespread dissemination of his thought and spirituality and also provide a stimulus to further translation of his writings into English. These latter are now being brought out in Italian, many of them for the first time, and it is our devout hope that the way is now open to further study, discussion, and deepening of the Lanterian spirit. Msgr. Cristiani's life is derived from the large collection of documents, published by the Sacred Congregation of Rites in 1945, with a view to the beatification of Father Lanteri. No doubt some things in his biography will have to be revised over the course of time, but his small book remains the most readable life in either Italian or French. Thus, it deserves to be known in English, especially now that the Oblates of the Virgin Mary, Father Lanteri's congregation, have established themselves in the United States. For the information of American readers we have included two appendices, one providing an account by Father Paolo Calliari, O.M.V., of Father Lanteri's early ministrations to the United States and the other giving a short sketch of the Oblates' formation program in Italy and the United States.

Our especial thanks go to the translators Mr. Keith Mayes and Mrs. Madeleine Soudée and to the Daughters of St. Paul, who in this and so many other respects have generously given our community their invaluable aid. To the many members of the international Oblate community who have had a hand in the production of this volume we also owe a large debt of gratitude.

Oblates of the Virgin Mary
Boston, Mass.
October 1980

A CROSS
FOR NAPOLEON:

THE LIFE OF
FATHER BRUNO LANTERI
(1759-1830)

CHAPTER I

CHILDHOOD—EDUCATION —VOCATION

A Fine Family

Cuneo is today a charming little Italian city of about 40,000 inhabitants and the seat of a bishopric since 1817. Under Napoleon it was the chief town of the French department of Stura, from the name of the river which waters the town. In the direction of France, to the west, rises the gigantic arc-shaped barrier of the ever-snowy Alps. Two hundred years ago, Cuneo was already a populous and prosperous township and was part of the Kingdom of Sardinia.

On the twelfth of May, 1759, there was born at Cuneo a child who was baptized, at 8 p.m. the same day, Pio-Bruno-Pancrazio. He was the seventh child and was to be followed by three more. His father, Pietro Lanteri, was a physician. His mother, Margarita Fenoglio, was a true servant of God and a wife worthy of the benevolent Doctor Lanteri.

The Lanteri family came from the little town of Brigue-Maritime which became part of the French state through the Franco-Italian treaty of 1947. The grand-father of Bruno was a notary in Brigue. Bruno's father, after studying medicine, came to set up a practice in Cuneo and very quickly gained a reputation for knowl-edge, professional skill and great Christian charity. What finer title can there be for a doctor than "father of the poor" which public gratitude bestowed on him as had been the case, in the early sixteenth century, with Antonio-Maria Zaccaria, the founder of the Barnabites?

Nevertheless the Lanteris' home had not lacked difficulties. Death repeatedly struck the family. The first three children, a girl and two boys, died young. Later two more, a boy and a girl, were to die. And the mother herself, scarcely 30 years old, died on July 19, 1763, while giving birth to a tenth child. She left three sons and two daughters. Let it be said at once that the three sons received Holy Orders. As early as 1770 Giuseppe Lanteri, who seems to have been five years older than Bruno, entered the Conventual Minors (Franciscans), and Giuseppe-Tomasso, the last-born, became a Barnabite in 1783 and died in August 1823.

Bruno Lanteri was only four years old when he lost his mother. Much later, when he was in his sixties, his eyes filled with tears when he told the story, and he used to say to his disciples and friends:

"I have had scarcely any mother but the Blessed Virgin Mary and I never received anything but comfort from such a good Mother!"

Early Education

It seems that Bruno was the favorite son of the children left Pietro Lanteri after the death of his wife. What is certain is that he guided him closely in his early studies and concentrated all his affection on him. Bruno became the doctor's almost inseparable companion. From him he learned, as did his brothers and sisters, not only the joy of prayer and of the most tender devotion to the Madonna, but also the rudiments of profane knowledge. He early showed a wonderful penchant for reading. Intellectual exchange was constant between father and son. "We studied with my father," he was later to say, "even at the table!" The child was gifted. His intelligence showed itself first, no doubt, by his incessant stream of questions. He wanted to know everything and to understand everything. He felt compelled to question his father about everything he read. In fact, Bruno preferred books to toys. Delighted by his son's inclinations, the father never tired of cultivating such promising talents. And like all fathers he was already making plans for his son Bruno. What should be done with him? The best way to find out was to ascertain his innate aptitudes. The child showed rare ability in mathematics. That was all his father needed to dream of making him a learned man, perhaps a university professor, a man called to distinguish himself in the sciences. The father himself at this time, around 1773, was becoming known in his profession for his useful and scholarly writings.

It goes without saying that Bruno, so well educated by his father, nonetheless followed the courses given at the school in his native town. He was an industrious and exemplary student. He detested diversions and time lost, and the documents we have on this period of his life declare that only three houses existed for him: the church, the house of God; the school, the house of learning; and his father's house. He was not seen anywhere else.

First Communion and Confirmation

Our sources inform us that Bruno received the sacrament of Confirmation on November 28, 1772, from the hands of Msgr. Ignaccio Gautier, Bishop of Iglesias, and, on this occasion, delegated to administer Confirmation by the bishop of Mondovi, on which Cuneo then depended.

Bruno was thirteen and a half. This age makes us stop and think. There is no mention in our sources of the child's First Communion. It is likely that it preceded Confirmation by a short time. From our present-day point of view it occurred rather late. The wise decrees of Pope St. Pius X have introduced very different practices in the Church. Everyone knows that, to the mind of the pious Pontiff, it was a question of reacting against the remains of Jansenism which continued among us. Bruno Lanteri was later on to be a resolute and intelligent opponent of Jansenism. But he seems to have been influenced by it despite himself, not only in the delay of his First Communion and his Confirmation, but even in a state of mind which he would find it hard to correct later on. Indeed it is surprising to find, shortly afterwards, in his private notes about his resolutions in preparation for Holy Orders, this sentence which has a distinct tinge of Jansenism: "Very few save themselves: that is why, if I wish to save my soul, I must mold myself after this minority, and when something seems difficult to me, if the minority does it, I must do it too, if I wish to be saved."

This preoccupation with the "minority of the elect" is very much in the spirit of the times and reveals a Jansenist atmosphere, a rather black pessimism, concerning human destiny and the restrictiveness of divine grace!

But we shall soon have to return to this topic in more detail.

Try-Out with the Carthusians

When Bruno Lanteri received the sacrament of Confirmation in 1772, his older brother, Giuseppe, had already left his father's house two years before to become a Franciscan. We do not know what thoughts this example stimulated in Bruno. The question of choosing a career had not yet arisen for him, and we have said that his father already envisaged him as a professor of mathematics. But as the years passed, Bruno had also to ask himself what road to follow. And it was not a casual decision that he declared one day to his dear father. It was in 1776; he was only 17. Deep in his heart he must have had serious debates with himself. Since we know that shortly afterwards he had and wanted constantly to have in mind the example of the elect—the small number of those who save themselves—and not that of the majority, we suppose that it was his great concern about salvation which suggested that he should in his turn, like his brother, join a religious order. But which one should he choose? Not far away was a Carthusian house, that of *Chiusa di Pesio.* To become a Carthusian was truly to copy the "minority." Did he not bear the name of Bruno—the name of the great founder of the Carthusians? Was this not an indication of the divine will?

Whether it was for these reasons or for others at which one might guess, it is certain that one fine day he confided his generous plan to his father. It is not hard to imagine the surprise and grief of Dr. Lanteri. What! Providence had taken away his wife, had taken five of his ten children, had led his eldest remaining son to a monastery. Now his Bruno was at stake, a son so gifted, so pious, so intelligent, and on whom he had focused all his hopes; it was his Bruno who spoke of burying himself in a Carthusian monastery!

Pietro Lanteri was, however, too Christian, had taken too much care to instill in his children piety and complete submission to divine wishes, to revolt against a vocation which displayed itself so forcefully and clearly. He decided, therefore, to take his son to the neighboring Carthusian monastery himself, thus treading underfoot all the fine plans he had made for the young man.

But this experience of monastic life was not to succeed. Bruno was a delicate and frail child. His courage was greater than his physical strength. The prior of the Carthusian monastery received him kindly and agreed to accept him as a postulant. But he did not take long to realize that Bruno was not fitted for the harsh Carthusian life. He judged that it was not even worthwhile for him to wear the holy habit. He explained to Bruno that he would not be able to keep the holy habit if it were given to him, and that the will of God, undoubtedly, was that he should return to his father's house. The Lord was satisfied with a pious intention. And the father and son had, in the circumstances, competed in generosity towards God. Abraham was ready to sacrifice his son, but his sacrifice was accepted by heaven in a more perfect way. Dr. Lanteri had also offered his Isaac, but his offering was to be completed in a different, though no less fine, manner.

Priestly Vocation

Bruno Lanteri had finished his studies and even, it appears, his course in philosophy. Once back home, he was all the more anxious to choose the right road, which he knew to be the way of sacrifice, of giving one's self, the way of total consecration to his God. Since the Carthusians were barred to him, he did not seek to enter another regular order. But a career in the Church remained open to him. For many at this time it was an envied, honored career, open even to the highest human aspirations, that is to say great dignities, benefices which were more or less opulent, but almost always comfortable. Bruno Lanteri, however, because he was already, as we believe, permeated by the necessity to hold to the "straight and narrow path," as his attempt to become a Carthusian seems to show, must have sworn to himself to follow an ecclesiastical career in a way utterly different from the majority. He desired neither honors nor riches. What he sought above all was the glory of God and his own salvation. We must believe that all this was discussed at leisure in Pietro Lanteri's home. Father and son agreed once again. It was decided that Bruno would ask his bishop, of Mondovi, for permission to wear clerical dress. We have the bishop's reply. It mentions the postulant's fulfillment of the necessary conditions: "legitimate birth, sufficient education, purity of morals, and a pious desire to sanctify oneself in the ecclesiastical status." And it grants him the requested permission on September 17, 1777.

At the University

In our days things would happen a little differently. A young man who wishes to receive Holy Orders approaches the superior of the seminary and, if he is accepted by him, enters it at the beginning of the academic year. It is only at the seminary that one takes the cassock, either on entry or after a period fixed by the diocese's practice.

In Bruno Lanteri's time, postulants took the cassock first, with the bishop's consent, then prepared for Holy Orders by studying theology, either in a seminary or at the university.

Children from comfortable families who were able to meet their living expenses usually chose this second route, which was more distinguished and could offer great advantages for those in uncertain health. This was the case with Bruno Lanteri. His father therefore thought that he should not go to the seminary but follow the courses of the theology faculty at some nearby university.

It seems that the father's first choice was the University of Pavia. He would have been influenced in this direction by the great reputation of a professor at that town's Atheneum, who was soon to have control of university studies: Pietro Tamburini (1739-1827), the recognized chief of Italian Jansenism. He was an extremely erudite man who published extensively, but who was, under the influence of Illuminism, completely infected with the doctrines of Balus, Jansenius, and

Quesnel, which he was to carry to triumph in 1786 at the famous Synod of Pistoia, of which he was the moving spirit with the collaboration of Scipione de' Ricci, the local bishop.

That Pietro Lanteri should have thought of confiding the future of his son to such a man would indicate a rather extensive ignorance of the serious debates which were tormenting the Church then. But this ignorance is only too excusable in a pious layman, especially at that time. Whatever the case may be, it was a remarkable grace that the young Bruno should not go to Pavia but be sent instead to Turin, which happened to be closer, and where, as we shall see, Providence arranged for him to meet a most reliable guide and most enlightened friend to prepare him for his sacerdotal life.

So it was decided that he would audit the theology courses of the university of Turin.

The expression "audit" is not completely accurate. If the future priest was not required to go to the seminary, he was nonetheless subjected to certain precise rules.

An instruction of Pope Benedict XIV, dated January 6, 1742, addressed to the bishops of the Kingdom of Sardinia, required that clerics not residing at the seminary must be listed among the clergy of a given church and be members of the staff of that church.

In Turin there were three "clergies" which students of theology were licensed to join. We do not know which church Bruno joined. But it is easy to imagine the risks to which he was exposed in the capital of the Kingdom, when he lived there, scarcely 19 years old, with almost complete freedom, lodging in a private house, and obliged only to be faithful in his studies and at the offices of the parish of his choice.

All the same, there was never any question of real dangers as to his private conduct. The only danger he would later denounce was the peril of Jansenism.

To understand properly this peril, as he had to face it, we must depict the intellectual and sprriritual atmosphere of the time, which had prevailed since the middle of the century in a good part of the clergy, the aristocracy and the people of Piedmont. Piedmont was undergoing the influence of French thinking. But Jansenism and Gallicanism displayed special nuances in Sardinia. The members of the clergy and the people with influence in the Kingdom professed very pronounced anti-Roman tendencies. A spirit of moral rigorism was spreading in the parishes. Its excessive demands cast into unbelief all those who felt themselves incapable of bearing so oppressive a yoke. Documents of the time tell us that books were circulating which discouraged the faithful from attending the sacraments, on the grounds that they were unworthy, discouraged them even from communicating at Easter, and suggested that they should die without receiving Extreme Unction. Pious Christians were also exhorted to give up traditional reverence for the saints, their images and their relics, the recitation of the rosary, the kissing of the crucifix and enrollment in devotional societies. Priests were warned not to permit unusual sermons in their churches, but to confine themselves to the Word of God, to the undecorated reading of the Sacred Scriptures. As for confessors, they were never to pardon mortal sins, and only very rarely venial sins, if penitents underwent lengthy trials.

Such a situation makes one think one is dreaming. But a contemporary, I. B. Biancotti, who knew Father Lanteri well, and was, from 1862 to 1870, to be the Father Superior of the Congregation of Oblates Father Lanteri founded, describes the spiritual climate in which Father Lanteri began his studies around 1778 in a report Biancotti wrote in 1846-1847.

Father Lanteri himself, while combatting the theology professed around 1817 by the Piedmontese theologian Salina, was to write: "Young priests are infected with Jansenism by means of the treatise *On Grace* and by the tone which prevails among the most serious and respected priests. Other priests are completely ignorant of what Jansenism is. They are tainted by it to the degree that they do not recognize it as a heresy and by virtue of the exaggerated rigorism which they profess."

Thus what he said in notes dating from a little after 1818 was already broadly true of the University environment of Turin in 1778. Jansenism had penetrated everywhere thanks to propaganda from beyond the Alps by means of "good books." "Good books" were thought to be only the Jansenist works coming from France. Let us keep this phrase in mind for it will help us to understand better the character of Father Lanteri's action. Convinced that the evil had come from "good books," he was to oppose the "good books" of Jansenism with the "good books" of anti-Jansenism.

But it is clear that he himself suffered for a time the assaults of Jansenism that were in the air, and that he had to struggle to escape them.

The Jansenist Temptation

On this delicate point we have the evidence of Father Giuseppe Loggero, who had been his penitent, his confidant, and his secretary for many years. Father Loggero wrote his account in 1840, ten years after the death of this Servant of God.

"Having been sent to the Royal University of Turin, to do his theological studies, he associated with a priest who did his best to win him to Jansenism.

"To this end he recommended to him and supplied him with Arnauld's book on *Frequent Communion*, the works of Nicole and others of the same type. Father Lanteri thought it an unusual grace of the Lord to have been enlightened about these questions; that he had recognized the falsity of these doctrines; that afterwards he had avoided the company of this priest; and that he had recognized the necessity of holding fast to the doctrines of the Roman Catholic Church, in order not to fall into error."

This text is categorical, and is not the only one. At the beginning of May 1838, Canon Luigi Craveri, who also knew Father Lanteri well, wrote an account of him. He states that Father Lanteri tried in vain to convert to the true doctrine that very man who was trying to lead him into Jansenism, but that having failed in this effort he broke off relations with him.

But if we believe Canon Craveri, our young student for some time shared the strictest opinions about Christian morality, and he was steered away from them only by meeting several wise people who expounded the Church's true doctrine to him. Craveri says outright that Bruno Lanteri "abandoned as a result of reasoned conviction, the rigorist system in order to embrace the doctrine derived from the decisions of the Holy Catholic Church, and the more benign opinions upheld by Catholic authors for the greater good of souls and the glory of God."

If Lanteri "abandoned" rigorism, that means that he had followed it up to that point. And that is exactly what we already deduced from his phrase about "the minority of those who are saved." He had to make a great effort to disgorge the Jansenist poison he had been absorbing, unconsciously, since his childhood.

But what Canon Craveri also teaches us, along with all the other witnesses of the life of Father Lanteri, is the names of those who succeeded, through God's grace, in saving the young student from his error and in bringing him, bag and baggage, if we may say so, into the opposite camp.

The details we have given here are far from insignificant. They help us, to some extent, to estimate the intensity and violence of the battles which raged over souls in those days. Because all this is remote from us, it is hard to understand it correctly. But it is clear that at this turning-point in Father Lanteri's career we find ourselves confronted by a direct continuation of the Port Royal heresy, which we described summarily in a recent small book.[1]

---

1. L. Cristiani, *The Port Royal Heresy*, Paris, Fayard, 1955.

CHAPTER II

FATHER DE DIESSBACH AND BRUNO LANTERI

A Trainer of Souls

The man who did most to save Bruno Lanteri from Jansenist rigorism and who at the same time exercised the most profound and decisive influence on his whole life as a priest and as founder of the Congregation was Father de Diessbach, a Jesuit, or rather, at that time, an ex-Jesuit, who had lived in Turin since the suppression of the Company in 1773 by Pope Clement XIV.

Who was this mysterious man? Where did he come from? How did he acquire the marvelous power which everyone recognized in him and which identified him, as had been the case with St. Gaetan of Tiene, as an admirable "hunter of souls"?

Few men exercised a happier influence at that time in Turin, and later in Vienna, Austria. Father de Diessbach was a "trainer" in every sense of the term. And it was in meeting him and by virtue of his lessons that Bruno Lanteri became one in his turn.

Nikolaus-Josef-Albrecht de Diessbach was born in Berne on February 15, 1732. He was 17 years older than Bruno. He belonged to a Swiss noble family, and on February 25, 1732, was baptized a Calvinist in the religion of his native town. At about the age of 15 he had, like so many of his fellow countrymen, entered the service of the King of Sardinia. He joined a Swiss regiment commanded by one of his uncles. Soon he had won the rank of captain.

Until then nothing suggested what he would one day become. No doubt he had come to detest Calvin and Calvinism, but that had not in any way directed him towards Catholicism, although, through his profession, he lived in Catholic surroundings. He had indeed fallen, like so many others in his time, the time of Voltaire and the Encyclopedists, into total incredulity. Since he was, however, by nature straight and true, he had not propagated impiety. No doubt he thought that the religion he did not accept for himself might be good for others.

Captain de Diessbach was a man of high society, a fine speaker, elegant and distinguished in his manners. Finding himself garrisoned at Nice, he was received by the best families in the town. And it was just here, in one of these families, if one may say so, that he found his "road to Damascus."

As if by chance there fell under his eyes, at the house of the Spanish consul, M. de Saint-Pierre, a book in which he delighted and which enlightened him so effectively on the Catholic faith that he converted completely. To make his *abjuration* he went to Turin. This conversion, which occurred in 1754, attracted enough attention for King Carlo-Emanuele to be informed of it. The King wanted to see him and was so impressed by his appearance and talents that he not only gave him command of a Sardinian regiment but entrusted him with the military education of his son, the future Vittorio-Amedeo III.

Diessbach had not, however, forgotten the house of M. de Saint-Pierre in Nice, where he had received a welcome so memorable and beneficial for his soul. As M. de Saint-Pierre had a daughter whose charms had perhaps contributed, indirectly, to his conversion, he asked for her hand in marriage. The marriage took place in 1755. Humanly speaking, happiness seemed to smile on the brilliant 23-year-old colonel! Alas! all the joys of this world are fragile. Three years later, in 1758, Diessbach lost his beloved wife, who left him a little daughter. Broken by grief, but consoled by the faith which had become all-powerful in his heart, he confided his child to the Sisters of the Visitation in Nice and decided to consecrate himself to the Lord by entering the Society of Jesus, although it was then already the object of fierce attacks by the Jansenists and all those who were called *regalists*, because of their hostility to Rome and their pronounced tendency to statism.

Jansenists and regalists were one day to be the great adversaries of Diessbach. For the moment—we are in 1759—he entered the Jesuit novitiate in Genoa. From the novitiate he passed to the scholasticate, to do his theological studies, and finally was ordained priest on September 22, 1764, by Most Rev. de Montenach, bishop of Lausanne and Geneva.

Diessbach was 32. He had already coped with many vicissitudes. He had known all ranks of society and his experience of men and life was great. Converted by a good book, he knew the power of the press in the life of his time. He would never forget his personal experience of it.

The First Works of Diessbach

A month after his ordination as a priest, Father de Diessbach left Switzerland at the request of his Jesuit superiors to go to Milan. That was where he waged his first battles for the Company. From Milan he had gone to Turin in 1771. But in the meantime the storm had battered the Company, sensational indictments had been brought against them, in France, in Portugal, in most

Catholic countries. They had been expelled everywhere. Vainly seeking refuge, they retreated to the Papal States. Royal diplomacy besieged the Court of Rome to have the Pope in person pronounce the Company's suppression. All these combined efforts finally led Pope Clement XIV, yielding to a pressure that had become intolerable, to destroy the Society by the brief *Dominus et Redemptor*, on July 31, 1773. By an incredible paradox the Jesuits survived for a while only in the states of the King of Prussia, Frederick II, and even longer in those of Catherine, Empress of all the Russias!

Everywhere else, ex-Jesuits, secularized where they were, devoted themselves to the various ministries people were kind enough to grant them. Their activity, which to some extent had gone underground, was all the more vigorous and fruitful. That is why they earned the restoration of their Order, pronounced officially by Pius VII on August 7, 1814.

Father de Diessbach is a good example of this extraordinary survival, despite the odious persecution of which the Jesuits were victims.

He found himself, as we have said, in Turin when the Order was suppressed. He remained there. He was known as a preacher. He spoke easily and could preach equally well in French, in Italian and in German. To his ministry as a preacher, he added that of writer, of a propagandist for sound doctrines through well-chosen books, in a word, as we have said, of a "hunter of souls."

He had no difficulty understanding that it was necessary to fight on two fronts. It was a matter of driving back incredulity and atheism, on the one hand, and Jansenism and regalism on the other. By his speech and his pen, Father de Diessbach spent himself without counting the cost. His writings, which are apologetic and ascetic for the most part, form a long list in the *Library of the Company of Jesus* established by Sommervogel.

As was natural, supporters came to him in sufficient numbers for him to found in Turin a pious Catholic Association to distribute sound books.

We shall see this Association develop under his direction and expand greatly under Bruno Lanteri's direction.

The latter, having come to Turin to do his theological studies, could not fail to come to know a man as active and talked about as Father de Diessbach. This eminent apologist, for his part, desired nothing more than to meet young students. As we have said, a battle of unbelievable ferocity was raging around them. The evolution of Lanteri, passing from the somber rigorism of the Jansenists, of whom he had been unaware until then, to the serene and consolatory doctrines of sound theology, provides us with a good example of these battles where the stakes were the souls of priests.

At the time when Bruno Lanteri came to Turin, probably in 1778, Father de Diessbach had just suffered a dreadful trial. His only daughter, who had resided with the Sisters of the Visitation, and had become a religious, had died there, a year after making her profession, on February 9, 1777. For her father the grief had been immense. His grief and the weariness resulting from so much hard work had made him ill. But nothing could crush the courage of this valiant athlete. We can be sure that for him it was consolation of the highest kind to conquer such an ardent, serious and committed young co-worker as Bruno Lanteri. Several pieces of evidence portray Diessbach and Lanteri, in intimate conversation, spending part of their nights discussing about God, prayer, errors and current problems, the doctrines of grace, and doing so until one and sometimes two o'clock in the morning! Lanteri no doubt had not given in without a struggle. We have seen that he had "through conviction" abandoned rigorism. But once convinced, Lanteri was not a man of half-measures. He went to the root of the thought of his new intellectual and spiritual director. Canon Craveri names among the participants in these memorable discussions with Diessbach a Father Bianchi and other "learned religious,"as he puts it. It goes without saying that the ex-Jesuits liked to meet and that in this mighty and absorbing conflict they were on the same side.

So in writing about the sacerdotal formation of Bruno Lanteri we are aware that we write a lively page of the religious history of the time just before the French Revolution.

But before tackling this part of our hero's life, we must indicate hurriedly how Father de Diessbach ended his career.

Journey to Vienna

One of Father de Diessbach's characteristics which he would transmit to his dear disciple Bruno Lanteri was to keep very well informed about current events and to read newspaper reports attentively to this end. He had a special skill, according to Bruno Lanteri himself, of grasping at once in daily events what related to the glory of God. And as soon as this glory seemed to him to be at stake, "he omitted nothing that could advance it." He did noᵼ hesitate to "undertake, despite his infirmities, very long journeys, even without any money, trusting entirely to divine Providence," for the success of his efforts.

In his apostolate he had the magnificent instinct of the true soldier who runs immediately to the most endangered point in the line, as soon as he hears the cannon's roar!

We see this when Pope Pius VI felt obliged to go personally to Vienna to negotiate with the Emperor Joseph II. What happened then in Father de Diessbach's heart? It is easy for us to guess from the facts. He hastened to rush to Vienna, taking with him his most faithful disciple, Bruno Lanteri.

"We have to go to Vienna," he must have told him, one morning early in 1782. "And you must come with me!..."

The young cleric, who had shortly before become a deacon, but was not yet a priest asked: "But what's going on?"

"The Sovereign Pontiff has to go to Vienna to negotiate with the Emperor. In the years he has reigned alone, Joseph II has not refrained from doing things contrary to the rights of the Church, and that without any prior understanding with the Holy See. Regalism is stronger in the Emperor's spirit than Catholic faith. As long as his mother, the Empress Maria-Theresa, lived, she kept him within the bounds of his duty to submit to canon law. But since she died, in 1780, he has not stopped affirming his absolutist pretensions. Helped by his ministers, Kaunitz and Cobenzl, he has put his hand on the Church in Austria. The Emperor alone is to decide ecclesiastical matters exactly like civil matters. He distributes even great benefices as he chooses without reference to Rome. He forbids the religious of various Orders who live in his states to have any dealings with their superiors outside the country. He requires an oath of loyalty of his bishops, just as the Kings of England do with Anglican bishops.

"He requires all documents of the Holy See to be submitted for his censorship before publication and before becoming law in his states. He has suppressed contemplative religious Orders on his own authority, allowing only those which are engaged in works of charity or public instruction. He arrogates the right to dispense monks whose way of life he has condemned from monastic vows, and to secularize them that way. As for the belongings of the orders he dissolves, he doesn't hesitate to have them administered by the state for its own profit. The Pope has protested again and again in vain. The Emperor, steeped in the anticanonical maxims of Richerism, which they call Gallicanism in France, refuses to listen. He is leading the Church in Austria to a kind of de facto schism, while proudly glorifying himself as wishing only the well-being of the Church and of the souls under his authority.

"The Sovereign Pontiff is going to Vienna to explain his duties to him, to bring him back to the great doctrine of Catholic unity of which Rome is the center and the Pope the guardian. But what kind of welcome will he get? Will faithful Catholics gather, pull themselves together, to show their obedience to the Pope, to let him see their filial affection, to escape the evil influences of regalism and put pressure on the hostile forces by the unanimity of their adhesion to the Pope?

"That is an urgent task for us. So let's go to Vienna. I'm already known there. I shall find support. We shall circulate a pamphlet I've written, entitled *What Is the Pope?* We will encourage the zeal of true Christians with all our power, and shall erect a barrier against the enemies of the Holy See!..."

In one form or another, such must have been the words of Father de Diessbach, just before leaving for Vienna. The situation was indeed so grave that Bruno Lanteri remained silent about the University courses he still had to follow, while promising himself to come back as soon as possible to complete his preparation for the priesthood.

In truth, Father de Diessbach's choice of Bruno for the mission he intended to fulfill in Austria is a striking proof of his confidence in him, of the high esteem in which he held his talents, of the affection he felt for him.

The Stay in Vienna

So the two friends went. They arrived in Vienna a month before the Pope. They had time to prepare minds for this august visit. Surely it was in part due to them that Pius VI found a triumphant welcome everywhere on his journey. The piety of the faithful was moving and enthusiastic everywhere. The great political problems by which the Church was so cruelly divided went over the heads of simple Christians. The mere name of the Pope aroused enthusiasm. But if the intense activity of Father de Diessbach and his disciple Lanteri was not fruitless, it changed nothing in the state of mind prevailing in the official spheres of the Austrian court. The Emperor gave the necessary orders so that the reception of the Pope would be outwardly impeccable, but, carefully sustained by his ministers, he held obstinately to his positions. The discussions took place from March 23 to April 22, 1782. The Pope vainly used all arguments to make the Emperor bend and to destroy his prejudices. He gained nothing, or at any rate the few concessions that were made to the Pope—regarding the rigor of the imperial approval demanded of pontifical documents before publication in Austria, if they should involve dogmatic definitions; regarding the circulation of the Bull *Unigenitus* against Jansenism; and regarding the misappropriation of benefices in Lombardy—these concessions, we say, were scarcely other than empty formulas. Joseph II has had the sad glory of giving his name to the regalism by which he was so permeated. *Josephism* is a kind of reinforced Gallicanism. It is a variety of *Richerism,* and shortly afterwards appeared as *Febronianism.* All the royal courts were more or less seriously contaminated by it then and it was the Josephist spirit that was to be found, soon afterwards, in France, in the famous *Organic Articles,* improperly appended by the French Government to the Convention of the Concordat.

Time Well Spent

Bruno Lanteri, with his friend Father de Diessbach, had found himself constantly embroiled in ideas in Vienna. While in the official discussions doctrines were clashing without appreciable change, one can well imagine that tongues were working busily in the salons, in the cafes, everywhere that people gathered. Regalist ideas were represented by a secular priest, Josef Valentin Eybel (1741-1805), already excommunicated for his anti-Roman theories at the University of Vienna, but saved by the Emperor and placed in charge of the administration of ecclesiastical matters. He too, in reply no doubt to Father de Diessbach's pamphlet, published a tract called *What Is the Pope?* which was put on the Index by a papal brief in 1786.

Taking part in these discussions of canon law and high theology, our Turin student could well say that he was not wasting his time, even if he was missing his University courses. His whole life was to be dominated by those experiences. He would have two great enemies to fight: Jansenism, from the point of view of Grace, and regalism or Josephism, from the point of view of the Church's theology.

A fact which deserves all our attention and which is, to our mind, a good proof of the fruitfulness accomplished by Diessbach and Lanteri in Vienna, is that Diessbach, putting Lanteri in charge of organized works in Turin and Piedmont, decided, for his part, to stay in Vienna. He was thus affirming that he had a most promising field in which to work.

Without spending more time than is necessary on this episode, we must note that he continued to work in the Austrian capital until his death in 1798, without however denying himself journeys abroad in behalf of the *Christian Friendship*, of which he was the inspired founder and of which we shall speak in the next chapter.

Panoramic view of Cuneo. In the foothills of the Alps.

The Carthusian Monastery of Pesio Cuneo, Italy.

He had first created the *Christian Friendship*, a kind of secret society destined to propagate good ideas through good books, in Turin, and found nothing of greater urgency than to found it also in intellectual circles in Vienna. We have very good reason to think that this group, *Christian Friendship*, established by Father de Diessbach, was the source of the Austrian literary movement called "Austrian romanticism." It was Diessbach who aroused such talents as Franz Schmid's. Now, Franz Schmid was the confessor of St. Clement Hofbauer, and it was around this saint that such artists and writers as Müller, Veith, Schlegel, another Müller, Brentano and so on, were to gather. It is certain that Diessbach himself knew Clement Hofbauer, and although we cannot fix the date of their first meeting, we are inclined to place it in 1782, in which case Lanteri may well have seen him as well. But we know positively that Clement Hofbauer belonged constantly, from 1795 on, to the circle directed in Vienna by Father de Diessbach.

In 1796, Father de Diessbach was offered the episcopal see of Lausanne and Geneva, which he refused in all humility. Two years later he was at Fribourg in Switzerland when the French invaded. He worked without stint caring for the wounded, but despite his charity he was attacked in his very ministry by some French soldiers, beaten and stripped. Scarcely recovered from his injuries, he went back to Vienna for the last time. And it was there that he died on December 22 of that year. Baron Penkler, who was one of the most active members of *Christian Friendship*, had his body taken to the Maria Enzersdorf cemetery, and it was around his grave that all the great "Austrian romantics" and Clement Hofbauer himself wished to be buried.

Bruno Lanteri summarized the apostolate of this vigorous champion of Catholic truth in the following lines:

"To know good books on every religious subject, and to use all means to distribute them and have them read by all classes of society, was, if I dare say so, his passion. This was principally because of the great benefit he remembered having derived from them himself. His erudition was immense in this area and his judgment of admirable certainty, all aided by a marvelous memory."

It is this kind of apostolate, which we may call the apostolate of the good press, that we shall see develop in the vast organization of *Christian Friendship*, with which the next chapter will deal at length. It was there in particular that Bruno Lanteri would begin to show his ability and to exercise that zeal for souls by which he felt more and more devoured.

CHAPTER III

THE CHRISTIAN FRIENDSHIP AND THE AA IN BRUNO LANTERI'S LIFE

Catholic Secret Societies

When one refers to a secret society, one thinks at once of freemasonry. Starting in 1719, it had spread in England and thence to France and other continental countries. But historic truth obliges us to recognize that Catholic secret societies antedated freemasonry. Everyone knows that one of these societies was that which developed in France to honor the Blessed Sacrament. In such a case there was a reason for secrecy. It kept the members, whose aim was their own purification and the glory of God, secure from sarcasm and worldly intrigues. Without being exactly secret societies, the *third orders*, beginning with the Franciscan, had given an example of assemblies without any publicity to the great Orders recognized by the Church. But in these secret societies, of which we shall speak, there was something more, in the sense that there was reborn in them, to some extent, that *Disciplina arcani*—secret discipline—that Christians in the first centuries of the Church practiced so rigorously, to protect the Eucharistic mystery from profanation by pagans, or, as was still said in St. Augustine's time, "non-initiates."

In the first rank of secret societies which served to sanctify the clergy in France in the seventeenth century we must point out the *Aa*.

Origins of *Aa*

Everything about the *Aa*, even its name, is mysterious. It was referred to by its adherents only by those letters. Historians wonder what they mean. Biographers of Bruno Lanteri, who have had to speak of it, thought, like Msgr. Ceretti, who wrote between 1841 and 1854, that they simply meant *Anonymous Association*, or *Anonymous Friendship*. This interpretation has been repeated in recent biographies of Bruno Lanteri, but it was not known to Lanteri himself and seems not to have been known before his time. Today opinion inclines to *Assembly of Associates* or *Association of Friends*, or something like that.

In any case it is of little importance.

In the beginning, the *Aa*, which played such a great role among the French clergy until the Revolution, appears as a secret Congregation among the great Marian Congregations of certain Jesuit colleges in France. The first traces of its existence go back to 1632. At that time six members of the Marian Congregation of the college of La Flèche—the one where Descartes was *educated*—met in great secrecy to study together the best ways of serving the Blessed Virgin and of observing the Congregation's rules more perfectly. So it has been possible to say of the *Aa* that it copied the Company of the Blessed Sacrament, but that its special object was the cult of Mary. The director of the Marian Congregation of La Flèche was at this time the famous Father Bagot. When informed of what was going on, he warmly approved of the fledgling association. That was what allowed enemies of the society to later on call its members derisively "Bagotians," while they called themselves the "Good Friends."

In 1643 one of the six members at La Flèche moved to Paris and there, with the agreement of the heads of the Marian Congregation at Paris' Clermont College, he introduced the practice of secret meetings among the most fervent members of the Congregation, as was the case at La Flèche. Father Bagot, who moved to Paris, took over direction of it in 1650. The Clermont College *Aa*, avoiding the noisy Paris White Rose Inn, where the college students met, found a more remote and peaceful meeting place in the rue Coupeaux.

Among the "Good Friends" of the rue Coupeaux was Vincent de Meur from Brittany, the man who later became superior of the Seminary of Foreign Missions in Paris. It was Vincent de Meur who in 1658 founded three important daughter groups of the *Aa* in Paris: in Toulouse, Bordeaux and Poitiers. In Toulouse his collaborator was Father Jean Ferrier, Director of the Marian Congregation at the Jesuit College. It seems that like de Meur most members of the *Aa* in Paris entered the Seminary of Foreign Missions. Whatever the case, it was the Toulouse *Aa* which was the most important center of the association. It was at Toulouse, also perhaps as a result of a suggestion by de Meur, that the *Aa* split into two sections, one reserved for the theology students and called the *Cleric's Aa* and the other intended for young men without a vocation to Holy Orders: the *Laymen's Aa*.

The foundation of the Seminary of the Foreign Missions, where Vincent de Meur was the superior from 1664 to 1668, is good proof of the apostolic spirit developed in the bosom of *Aa* in its two forms. The association worked enthusiastically both for the sanctification of its members—the *Good Friends*—and for the salvation of souls. The evidence so far collected shows us that the *Aa* existed in more than 30 towns in France, Canada, Italy,

Switzerland and Bavaria. According to Georges Goyau, the division of the *Aa* into two sections was carried out in Toulouse in 1676.

The *Aa* was introduced into Savoy by a fervent priest named Daguerre. It soon spread to Turin, through the efforts of one of its members named Murgeray. We speak of course of the *Clerical Aa,* of which Bruno Lanteri was one of the first members in Turin, as soon as it was founded. He remained one of its most fervent promoters, very probably until the day in 1811 when he was put under house arrest by Napoleon's order in the country at La Grangia. There is no danger of our being mistaken if we say that the *Clerical Aa* met his sacerdotal ideal and that the texts which tell us about the *Aa* teach us simultaneously about Bruno Lanteri's spirituality in the decisive years of his sacerdotal formation.

The Aims and Origins of *Aa*

We have several letters written by Chambery's *Aa* to that in Turin between 1785 and 1787, in which mention is made of Bruno Lanteri. But what we shall seek there in particular is the declaration of the objective and origins of the Association.

As for the objective, the following passage is perfectly clear: "*Aa,*" says a letter of 1787, "is a holy union of heart, body and spirit among people who wish to work seriously for their perfection and to contribute everything in their power to the sanctification of those who are preparing for the priesthood. Thus it would be false to think that one would gain much from it if one were satisfied with attending the weekly meetings, without setting one's shoulder to the wheel, without working to correct one's faults, to acquire the virtues which we lack, and without working to form subjects who may replace us and continue the work of God."

This is very clear. They wanted to become holy priests and wished to transmit the torch to succeeding generations.

Another letter—of 1785—will show us the springs at which such generous aspirations refreshed themselves.

"The *Aa*," says this letter, "is a fecund source of all goods: it is the tree God in His mercy planted in the Church to revive the almost extinguished zeal of His ministers. As far as that is concerned, France was happily the first to gather the fruits and to carry them to all parts of the world. How joyful heaven has been to see a country despoiled by heretics find people like de Meur, Boudon, Olier, Vincent de Paul, Bourdoise, Francis de Sales, La Serre, Dufaux, Lalannes, Monmorin, Benoît, Tessier, Tessiné, Blanca, Daguerre and so many other fervent subjects of the *Aa* who have revived the faith and ecclesiastical spirit, which were almost extinguished in vast and opulent European countries, in this elder daughter of the Church, as the Sovereign Pontiffs call it!..."

This list of "great men" venerated in the bosom of the *Aa*, even if it contains many names which no longer convey much to us, is extremely interesting. Again and again in the pages that follow we shall speak of the propagation of good books. But we nowhere find a catalog enumerating the good books in question. We can be sure that everything issuing from the pious people whose names we just read was welcomed in Turin, as elsewhere, with eagerness and enthusiasm. If we add to these names, and especially to that of Francis de Sales, who for a Piedmontese was a compatriot, that of Alfonso-Mario de Liguori, who was also an intrepid battler against Jansenism, rigorism and regalism, we shall have a fairly representative glimpse of what were called "good books" by the people around Bruno Lanteri.

But we shall see, in recalling the sources of the *Christian Friendship*, that people in Turin had not waited for the arrival of the *Aa* to enter on an exactly comparable course.

Christian Friendship

There are such obvious analogies between the French *Aa* and the *Christian Friendship* founded by Father de Diessbach in Turin that it is tempting to believe that the latter copied the former. Certainly the *Aa* is much older, but we cannot say with any confidence that it was known to Father de Diessbach when he created the *Christian Friendship*. Between the two there are the following resemblances: first the character of a secret society, then the identity of the aims—the sanctification of their members and expansion of the reign of God—finally the identity of means: regular meetings on the one hand and the distribution of "good books" on the other.

It is not impossible that Father de Diessbach knew something of the *Aa*, when he conceived his *Christian Friendship*. But it is just possible that a convergence of the methods and objectives of the two societies occurred without any influence by the older on the younger.

The *Christian Friendship* was proposed for the first time by Father Nicholas de Diessbach in his book: *The Catholic Christian irrevocably committed to religion through consideration of some of the proofs which establish its certainty.* In volume III of this work, published in Turin in 1771, he proposed a union of all friends of the Catholic religion to defend morality and dogma by means of a good press.

But so far this was only a seed planted in the ground. The seed developed. Meanwhile the Company of Jesus had been suppressed. Father de Diessbach had not slowed down his activity because of this. On the contrary, he used the liberty restored to him against his wishes to hurl himself into the struggle. The idea he had launched became concrete around 1776 in the institution of a "Pious Association" among Italian Catholics to favor publication and distribution of "good books." The base of the Association was to be Fribourg in Switzerland, but subscriptions were accepted in 31 bookshops in as many Italian towns. Subscribers were to receive six volumes each year.

The first distribution could not take place until 1778.

The first attempt gave Father de Diessbach the idea of a more concentrated work, with a more defined and richer target. Instead of committing themselves to subscribe to six "good books" a year, members of the new organization would work above all for the glory of God and for their personal sanctification. But they would also work at their apostolate through the press.

Father de Diessbach gave the new Association the fine name of the *Christian Friendship—Amicizia cristiana.* In the texts which refer to it, it is always called by the initials A.C.

The organization seems to have been formed in Turin between 1778 and 1780. That was exactly when Bruno Lanteri came to Turin for his theological studies. It is difficult to say exactly when he joined the *Christian Friendship.* But the preponderant role he was to play in it after 1783 leads us to believe that he joined the Association as soon as he met Father de Diessbach, in 1779.

He would work so well at *Christian Friendship* after returning from Vienna, in the absence of its revered founder, that we must study closely the nature and arrangement of this association. There we shall see the essential shape of Bruno Lanteri's apostolate, after his sacerdotal ordination.

But first we must say something about his ordination.

Bruno Lanteri and Holy Orders

Bruno, on arriving in Turin, had to be active on two fronts: theological studies and preparation for Holy Orders. The fact that he was busy in Father de Diessbach's work, far from raising an obstacle to pursuit of the two objectives, helped him enormously. He found in him a counsellor, a leader, a scholar of the first rank, consequently a guide and, if one dares say so, an excellent tutor for his courses at the university.

To speak first only of these courses, Bruno had serious difficulties with his sight, which he ruined early by his prolonged reading. He was seriously near-sighted and was to suffer from this all his life. So he found it hard to read the course-sheets which were distributed to students by professors. Later he had to say that he had learned his theology "more by my ears than my eyes." Not satisfied with giving all his attention to the lectures and explanations of the university's professors, he would stimulate discussion among his fellow students. He used these discussions to perfect his knowledge, with that attention to detail that we know he had in the sciences. And there can be no doubt that the long conversations he had, as we have said, with Father de Diessbach and other knowledgeable theologians until 1 or 2 a.m. must often have dealt with theological points that were the knottiest and most debated in those days. The result was excellent for, shortly after his return from Vienna, on July 13, 1782, he passed his examinations for a doctorate in theology. From that date, with his diploma, he held the impressive title: Lanteri the theologian! Indeed he is often referred to by this title in the archives which are before us. He is also often simply called "the theologian."

A little before he achieved his doctorate in theology, Bruno Lanteri had been ordained a priest, on May 25, 1782. But his progressive rise to this sublime dignity had taken place, in accordance with canon law, from his first tonsure, in October 1780.

The tonsure, in fact, is not an Order but merely a preliminary to Holy Orders. But Bruno Lanteri had to win a *title* for himself with a view to future ordinations, that is, a guarantee that he would as a priest possess decent means of existence. He had money. He obtained from his father the *constitution* of what is called, by canon law, a patrimonial title, which would allow him to live as a free priest, without being officially attached to any paid post. This qualification would give him great opportunies for personal apostolate. His patrimonial title is dated September 30, 1780, and shortly preceded his admission to the tonsure. He received Minor Orders in September 1781, was ordained sub-deacon on September 22 of that year, and, three months later, on December 22, was ordained a deacon. A few days afterwards he left for Vienna with Father de Diessbach. But he returned immediately after the departure of the Pope, to be ordained a priest, with a dispensation of 13 months for lack of age.

Servitude to Mary

In between these successive ordinations, on August 15, 1781, he had done something which shows us the depth of his Marian piety. He was then at Cuneo, in the midst of his family. In a fine outburst of fervor, he wrote the following pledge of consecration to the Virgin:

"Let all to whom these words shall come know that I, Bruno, sell myself as a slave in perpetuity to the Blessed Virgin Mary, our Lady, by a gift entirely pure, free and perfect, of my person and all my goods, so that she may use me as she pleases as my true and absolute mistress. But as I recognize myself unworthy of such a grace, I pray my holy guardian angel, St. Joseph, St. Teresa, St. John, St. Ignatius, St. Francis Xavier, St. Pius and

St. Bruno, to obtain for me from Mary most holy that she may deign to receive me among the number of her slaves. In faith whereof I sign: Pio Bruno Lanteri."

To the mind of the young cleric, this was a most grave and serious act. By it he vowed himself to an apostolate, without reserve or limit, under the patronage of Mary. Whence had such a thought come to him? We could believe, nowadays, that he was inspired by the famous work of St. Louis de Montfort: the *Treatise on True Devotion to the Blessed Virgin*, which has made the practice of slavery to Mary very widespread in spheres of Catholic piety. But the work of Louis de Montfort was not known then. As the saint had predicted, it was to remain buried in his papers until its discovery and publication, in 1842, 12 years after Bruno Lanteri's death. Thus we must rather seek the origin of this decision in the forms of devotion flourishing among members of the *Christian Friendship*, to which the pious cleric belonged. Through St. Francis de Sales, through Bérulle, through Boudon, a very strong spiritual current bore the faithful to devotion to the Virgin. Louis de Montfort found himself plunged in this same current, when he wrote the celebrated treatise we mentioned. This same current had touched a spirit as penetrating and ardent as that of Alphonsus de Liguori. In his book on the *Visits to the Holy Sacrament and to Most Blessed Mary*, published in 1749, and also in his *Glories of Mary*, in 1750, consecration to Mary was clearly suggested. Father de Diessbach may very well have advised his faithful disciple to make this solemn act, and the dedication that Dr. Lanteri had made of his son Bruno, after the death of his wife, prepared the young man for such a step.

In any case, this indicates how deeply the *Christian Friendship* aimed to work in depth in the spirits of its members. That brings us back to the study of the functioning of this providential association.

The Organization of Christian Friendship

The first aim of the *Christian Friendship* was to work for the glory of God, by making Him reign in the hearts of its members and, through them, in all whom they were capable of reaching. To that end, the members of the Association were to cultivate, with all their strength, the theological virtues, since it is through them that God is most honored: faith, hope and charity. As a practical way to do so, the *Christian Friendship* proposed to distribute good books.

The society was secret. It could count, therefore, only on limited numbers. With large meetings, secrecy is impossible. In each town, accordingly, the *Christian Friendship* restricted itself to 12 members, six of them men (priests or laymen) and six of them women. Among themselves the members called each other "the Friends." The inclusion of an additional member is provided for only in exceptional circumstances, and such an additional member would take no part in deliberations. For the exercise of his apostolate, each member should recruit "seekers," male or female, to serve as collaborators. All must be reliable people, of impeccable life, of high culture so far as possible, of disinterested and sincere zeal. Each of the six male members had a title and a position in the group. First came the *First Librarian*, who directed the group and had to have unquestionable competence in matters of literary production and librarianship. Next came the *Second Librarian*, whose duty was the entire administrative side of the *Friendship*, that is, purchases of books and the cost of distribution of good books. Third came the *Promoter*, whose job was to keep an eye on the offshoots of the *Friendship*, called *Colonies*, and on the discipline of the whole organization. The *Secretary* kept records of the facts or events which interested the *Friendship*. After him came the *Instructor*, who was responsible for the formation of aspirants or supernumerary members during their year of preparation. Finally, the *Missionary* was the executive agent of the *Friendship's* decisions and was to work for its growth in neighboring or even remote towns.

The women in the group had no specific task, but simply gave their advice in deliberations.

Spirituality

Capital importance in *Christian Friendship* was ascribed to the interior life and the quest for a high spirituality on the part of all members. Each of them, according to the Directory of Work, had to be able to say conscientiously: "I have no free or considered desire stronger, or even as strong, as that to have Jesus Christ reign in my soul and in those of other men through faith, hope and charity." Such a formula agrees so perfectly with the practice of the holy servitude to Mary, that we can regard it as certain that the dedication of Bruno Lanteri, which has been discussed already, is in complete conformity with the spirit of the *Christian Friendship*.

To accomplish their high ideal, the "Friends" committed themselves to receive the sacraments twice a month—which seemed a lot at the time—to devote themselves daily for at least half an hour to the holy exercise of prayer and spiritual reading, to make a spiritual retreat of eight or, at the very least, three days every year, and even, if it should prove possible, to retire occasionally into complete solitude, and finally to fast on various occasions and to practice profound devotion to the Sacred Heart of Jesus, Mary most holy, St. Joseph and Saint Teresa.

Each of them was in addition to know the "good books" thoroughly and to observe strictly the rules of the *Friendship*.

Rules of the Friendship

We know these rules. They involved vows, meetings, and care for a library.

Their vows were three, but were taken for only one year:

First was the vow never to read books prohibited by the Church, even if granted special permission. The only exception was for writers who had to refute evil doctrines.

Second was the vow to read spiritual works for an hour a week, books approved by the *Friendship*.

Third was the vow to obey the superiors of the *Friendship*.

In the beginning the meetings took place every week but later only every other week. They usually lasted two hours. They dealt with all the questions which interested the *Friendship*, beginning always with prayer and some spiritual reading. Votes were by secret ballot. Very occasionally there might be meetings called "charitable" (*de charité*), and all adherents of the *Friendship*, in whatever capacity, would take part, but no decision would then be reached.

The Library was of great importance in the existence of the *Friendship*. It was to be installed in a place adorned tastefully. In addition it was there where meetings were held. Books kept for the *Friends* were divided into three categories: polemical, ascetic, and literary. These works formed what was called the *permanent* library, that is, books that were not loaned out. Besides members of the *Friendship*, it was permitted to welcome to the library people who could be trusted, whether priests or laymen. In code, the library was called "the pharmacy."

But in addition to this permanent library, there were books meant to be loaned out. These were selected from those belonging to the main library in duplicate or triplicate. Some books were to be distributed free. Distribution of books was carried out either by the *Friends* themselves, or by collaborators whom we have called *Seekers*. The catalogue was carefully maintained and was not to receive any new book without its being examined privately by the *Friends* and being approved unanimously. It was divided into eight categories: 1. for people with doubts about religion because of lack of instruction; 2. for those who were in difficulties because of bad readings; 3. for those who were struggling against the passions and beguilements of the world; 4. for scrupulous people and those who felt discouraged; 5. for people aspiring to perfection; 6. for creation of a taste for good reading; 7. for those who knew themselves poorly; 8. for those devoted to study.

Two special catalogues contained only "very strong" books and "exquisite" books, that is, the ones most suitable to lead people to piety or to illumine the controversies of the day.

The *Friends* proposed to touch all segments of society. They forgot neither the poor, nor the sick in the hospital, nor people in prison.

Expansion of Christian Friendship

This organization, established in such detail and organized so powerfully, did not take long to spread outside Turin, where it had been born. We have seen that it developed in Turin between 1778 and 1780. Thereafter it gave birth to *daughter groups* in various cities in and outside Italy. Although we cannot date with certainty the foundation of the *Friendship* in each new town, it seems that it took root between 1783 and 1790, first in Milan, then in Fribourg in Switzerland, and finally in Paris. This last foundation is very interesting for our little religious history. Our sources tell us of a "Society of Good Books" in Paris at the end of the Revolution. It is overwhelmingly probable that this society was only a restoration of the *Christian Friendship*, transported from Turin to Paris, just before France's great political upheavals, that is to say, before 1790. If this conjecture is right, it would mean that the first works which brought Catholics together in France at the beginning of the nineteenth century would have originated in the admirable movement created by Father de Diessbach in Turin. We are sure in any case that he travelled to Paris to set his *Christian Friendship* going, as he had in Turin, then in Vienna in 1782, and in Fribourg in Switzerland. Among other centers of the *Christian Friendship*, set up between 1790 and 1803, we can list those of Augsburg in Germany, Florence, Rome and Warsaw. The *Christian Friendship* served educated and zealous Catholics everywhere as centers of activity with a view to Catholic restoration, after the great revolutionary and Napoleonic disturbances.

And it was in this sphere that Bruno Lanteri was called to exercise his apostolate immediately after his sacerdotal ordination, as we shall see in the next chapter.

CHAPTER IV

THE MINISTRY OF BRUNO LANTERI FROM HIS ORDINATION TO THE FRENCH OCCUPATION (1782-1798)

The New Priest

The priestly career of Bruno Lanteri divides naturally into three distinct periods. The first runs from his ordination to the French invasion, 1782 to 1798; the second covers the period of French occupation and runs to the fall of Napoleon, 1798 to 1814; the third and last extends from the 1814 restoration to Lanteri's death, 1814 to 1830. It is a curious, but fortuitous, coincidence that these three periods are of about the same length: each sixteen years.

We shall follow as closely as possible the sacerdotal activity of this servant of God.

As for the first period, we know he joined the *Christian Friendship* and we also know that this association had a goal, an ideal, means of action and methods of apostolate that we can only admire and approve from first to last. Yet it is not the beauty of an institution which we must consider, but rather the intelligence, fidelity and perseverance of the men who use it in their plans, and above all the purity of intention, the breadth of vision, which animate and inspire these plans.

For Bruno Lanteri we have an indication of vast and noble desires filling his soul in the act of dedication he had made of his person and his belongings to the Blessed Virgin, as her *slave*, which is to say in the purest French mystical tradition of which Bérulle had been a representative.

But what had become of his fine resolutions two years later, when he attained the priesthood?

This question is one of the most important we could raise. And we have a document which answers it with unmatchable clarity, the spiritual directory (for composing the Spiritual Exercises) which he compiled in the five months between his ordination to the diaconate and his attainment of the priesthood. He dated it at the beginning as of January 6, 1782, but he compiled it little by little, and finally pulled together the pages, of different sizes and with differing scripts, in a fascicle of 28 pages, which is the most complete thing we have to show the frame of mind in which he approached his sacerdotal ministry.

What strikes one at the first glance is that he refers constantly to the rules of the *Christian Friendship* on the one hand and of the *Aa* on the other. The two associations seem to him to converge on the same objective. He applies their principles to himself, and derives from them a complete plan for his life. And as he does not wish the plan to be confined to paper, he makes it his absolute rule to reread his resolutions every week until he is ordained priest.

What are these resolutions?

1. Never to omit meditation and to meditate methodically and faithfully.

2. To prepare in the evening before receiving the Eucharist and to use this preparation to visit the Holy Sacrament.

3. To practice a precise and certain method of confession, to leave nothing to routine, to chance, to the spur of the moment.

4. To try for a month to perform six acts of generosity each day, and to write them down; to make a point of always thinking, speaking and acting as the saints did, as is required by the spirit of the genuine ministry of God and the regulations of the "Good Friends" and "confederates," which means the people of the *Christian Friendship* and the *Aa*.

5. To meditate every two weeks on the true priestly spirit, according to the principles of the same associations.

6. To take whatever time is necessary to renew himself through the Spiritual Exercises in a good retreat.

7. To promulgate devotion to the Blessed Virgin on all occasions which may arise and especially when speaking in public.

Special Vocation

In this same directory, Bruno Lanteri does not limit himself to conformity, however edifying. No doubt he wanted to be faithful in every way to the *Christian Friendship* and the *Aa* and he spared no effort to enter fundamentally into the spirit of the two associations. Some passages in his directory, written in summary form, but sufficiently explicit for us to understand them, prove that he did not shrink from harsh penitential measures: mortification in his meals, scourging, an iron bracelet, once a week. Once he became a priest his daily timetable would be fixed without variation: each day, meditation, Mass, office of the breviary, spiritual reading, visit to the

Holy Sacrament, study, six acts of generosity, examination of conscience, voluntary denial at table, no useless thought, thinking only of God's service and the good of souls. "To think, speak and act always like a saint." To speak of God as soldiers speak of war, to be towards all people kind, smiling, faithful, magnanimous, simple, calm, joyous and compassionate.

But for him that was an ordinary vocation, open to every genuine priest. Was there not besides, for him, a special call by Providence? The most profound pages of his directory bear on this point. One sees to what degree this young priest was given to meditation and the inner life.

What happened to him in fact? He was a priest, but a *free priest*, and as he himself said, in a "state of complete liberty," that is, attached to no parish as a pastor or assistant, not tied down to any official task, but able to use his time and his means for the greater glory of God. What should he do to that end? What did God demand or expect of him? Such was the question he raised during a retreat.

"I can do no less," he wrote, "than confess that His divine Majesty wishes, in this circumstance, something special from me, a miserable sinner and His unworthy servant. I understand that particularly because of the special promptings His Majesty gives me from time to time, asking me to dedicate myself altogether to His Majesty's service and the salvation of souls...."

What God wanted he understood in this way: that he should sacrifice the liberty he had by vowing obedience to his director Father de Diessbach in everything: in all that concerned his soul; in all that concerned the glory of God and the good of souls. He renewed his vow of chastity, and his dedication to the practice of the spirit of poverty to the fullest extent possible.

He visibly sought to sacrifice himself. He had not been able to become a Carthusian, as he had wished when young, but he retained their spirit and ideal, that of the utter gift of self to God alone.

Diessbach's Reply

The vow of obedience to Father de Diessbach implies a correspondence between Lanteri and his spiritual director. But nothing remains of this correspondence. In any case, according to the rules of the *Christian Friendship*, it had to be secret and to be obscured in part by a code. But it is not hard to guess Father de Diessbach's instructions.

From Vienna he gave or rather confirmed the instructions which he must have issued many times to his dear pupil. In the first place, not to leave Turin, which would thus become his field of activity. Normally Bruno Lanteri, born at Cuneo in the diocese of Mondovi, was supposed to or at least could have returned to his original diocese and offered himself to his bishop to be assigned a ministry.

But even if he did not return to his diocese, other solutions were open to a "free priest" such as Lanteri. There was then no lack of priests whose career was spent in the cultivation of books or studies, even philosophy. Lanteri could have been another Muratori or Condillac. His biographers assure us that it was suggested that he should become the tutor of the son of the Duke of Modena, or even librarian of the duke's private library. But neither Lanteri nor Diessbach found it acceptable for a priest to seek out such advantageous benefices and the conveniences of life at court.

Bruno did not desire honors. Not only was he not interested in money, but he was inclined to give everything he possessed to the service of God and of souls.

The first decision taken, with the agreement of his director, was to remain in Turin. To do this he needed the consent of his bishop. He asked and obtained it without difficulty. Thus he obeyed the rules.

But what would he do in Turin? We know already. His basic activity would be with his cherished *Christian Friendship*. From the moment when Father de Diessbach stayed in Vienna, where he too had found an excellent theater for his apostolate, it was necessary to reorganize the direction of the *Christian Friendship* in Turin, which was the work's cradle. There was no question of confiding its direction to Bruno immediately, for he was only 23. Direction was conferred, with the title of "First Librarian," on Father L. Virginio, like Diessbach an ex-Jesuit, but also a friend, and even a compatriot, of Bruno. But Bruno came immediately after Father Luigi Virginio, with the title "Second Librarian." That at once gave him an enormous amount of work. It was his job to keep track of editions in the libraries, to know about new publications, to rout out "evil books" and to buy good new ones for the *Friendship's* library. Given the love of books he had felt since his childhood, this kind of work suited him wonderfully. We are sure that he devoted himself to it unstintingly. He was, in the full meaning of the term, the linchpin of the *Christian Friendship* in Turin, and as Father Virginio was often away to fulfill his personal ministry, since he went in particular to live for several years in Milan, where he created another section of the *Friendship*, the effective direction in Turin rested on Bruno's shoulders.

Towards the Direction of Souls

To be directing a *Christian Friendship*, while still so young, was already an achievement. But that could not satisfy the zealous ardor by which Bruno felt devoured.

Besides the duties of a pastor or assistant, there was more than one way to exercise a ministry. Most importantly, there were preaching, confession and the direction of souls. Here, too, Father de Diessbach must have given his opinion and advice. Bruno was not the sort of man to preach. He had a small voice, and was not strong. His biographers tell us constantly that he felt "pressure in the chest" which no doubt means that he had emphysema or even asthma attacks. In fact he would preach only very rarely in his life. His way would be completely different and would be nonetheless fecund. He would address small groups of listeners, gathered for the "Spiritual Exercises." Bruno Lanteri, we shall have to repeat, would be one of the specialists of his time in the famous Exercises of St. Ignatius.

But there could be no question for him of confining himself to preaching retreats, without directing souls. This he would be above all: a spiritual director, a remarkable confessor, a liberator of spirits tyrannized by Jansenist rigorism. It would be in this domain—that is to say, in the depths of the soul, so to speak—that he would obtain his greatest successes, and it would be there that he would exercise the greatest influence.

Therefore, a second decision of Father de Diessbach must have been that Bruno should prepare himself for the ministry of confessions. Of course he was a priest, but, according to the practice of the time, he was so far ordained only *ad missam.* Shortly afterwards he became a doctor of theology, but that was not sufficient according to prevailing canon law for him to be allowed to hear confession. Young priests, after ordination, went several years without hearing confession. Above all they had to study to be pastors and take an appropriate examination to receive power to administer the sacrament of Penance. We shall see later that Bruno Lanteri took great interest in young priests who had already left the seminary but were obliged to prepare for this pastoral examination, and in the meantime were set free in town at great risk to their sacerdotal virtue. He was not satisfied until he had contributed to the creation of an establishment to receive them, which would be called the "Convitto." But there was nothing of the kind in his time. He had three years of study ahead of him before the pastorate.

It was in this period that he suffered the death of his father. Good Dr. Pietro Lanteri, who had just given his last son, Giuseppe-Tomasso, to God, died at Cuneo on October 31, 1784.

As soon as his father was afflicted by his last illness, Bruno rushed to be with him. For three months he stayed by his bed; it was granted him to console and encourage this excellent father. Bruno's grief, at the death of such a beloved person, was immense. But what was most painful for him was to be hurled into the material worries of arranging the inheritance. Dr. Lanteri's fortune was relatively substantial for the time. It has been estimated at about 500,000 lira, which would be worth about $200,000 today. Even when this fortune had been shared equally among the five surviving children, Bruno's share remained considerable. But he showed how little attached he was to the things of this world. In Turin he had had to worry only about his priestly perfection. Was he now to be bogged down in calculations about rates of interest or in the administration of temporal goods? His friends in Turin needed him back. Bruno hastened to meet their desires, which he and his director, Father de Diessbach, shared. He succeeded in transmitting responsibility for these matters to a cousin named Pietro di Medici who deserved all his confidence. Freed of preoccupations of this type, he went back to Turin and continued his preparation for the pastoral examination. He passed this easily a year later and received an *aux fidex* of confessorship from the archbishop of Turin, Msgr. Costa di Arignano, on October 22, 1785.

He was authorized to reside in Turin, to exercise his ministry there, on the condition that from time to time on the demand of the archdiocese he would provide certification of his good behavior from the pastor of the parish in which he lived, or from the ecclesiastical authorities in places where he exercised his functions.

We possess a certain number of these certificates, and they have the advantage for us of stating his places of residence during the first years of his priesthood.

The first of these reports is dated October 20, 1785, two days before he received his certificate as a confessor. It was written by the pastor of St. Thomas of Turin. It declares that the priest Bruno Lanteri, native of Cuneo, has been living in the parish for five years—since 1780—and that he has always been noteworthy for the perfect regularity of his morals, his piety and his good example.

Two years later it was the bishop of Lausanne, Msgr. de Lenzburg, who gave him the warmest approval on May 19, 1787. We learn from this document that Bruno Lanteri had just made a stay of some length in Lausanne—very probably and almost surely to expand the *Christian Friendship*—and that he had shown himself to be a man "of good life, splendid conduct, and excellent doctrine." On which basis the bishop of Lausanne recommends him highly to all prelates, priests and others with whom the priest Lanteri may deal.

How He Spent His Time

It must be admitted that documents that would allow us to study closely Bruno Lanteri's activity are either lacking or extremely rare. What we know of how he spent his time, later in life, may help us to form an idea of how he spent the day. He was always so methodical and faithful to his resolutions that there is little risk of mistake in attributing this management of time to the first years of his priesthood.

The best and most recent of his biographers, Father Tomasso Piatti, tells us that he devoted seven hours to pious exercises, seven hours to rest, and ten hours to work.

These figures are eloquent and arouse more than one reflection. Let us consider first the seven hours spent in pious exercises. This is enormous, in relation to our normal practice. We consider a priest fervent and exemplary if he preaches, says Mass, recites his breviary, does not omit his rosary nor his visit to the Blessed Sacrament, and ends his day with solid spiritual reading. But let us calculate more exactly: all that takes only three or three and a half hours a day. With his seven hours of pious exercises, Bruno Lanteri can be numbered with the "giants of prayer." On the basis of the evidence, he must have multiplied his prayers, or prolonged his visits to the Blessed Sacrament, or devoted much time either to celebration of Mass or to recitation of his office.

If we pass from these seven hours to the seven hours he gave to sleep and meals, we can only find this time very limited. Surely he cannot have slept more than five or six hours a night. His meals too were hurried. He was granting nature only what he could not deny it without danger to his health, which was always poor.

Finally, ten hours of work are an impressive total. We know roughly what this work was: careful reading of good books, numerous notes taken while reading, preparation of instructions for retreats by small groups he gathered for the Exercises, visits to booksellers, careful preparation of meetings of the *Christian Friendship*, confession at regular times either in the church of his parish or in other churches open to his zeal, close study of the gazettes to keep up with events, among which in these

Panoramic view of Turin (Italy).

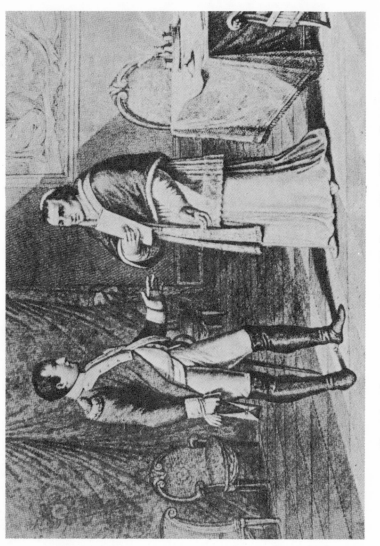

Napoleon's meeting with His Holiness Pius VII at Savona.

first years of Bruno's priesthood were some of resounding import, in that they heralded or carried out the French "Revolution." That was quite enough to fill one's days. Bruno was attentive to everything which affected God's glory. That is what he had admired in Father de Diessbach—he tells us so himself—and on this point he took care not to be unfaithful to so fine an example. His soul vibrated with everything that happened day by day. He took advantage of everything for his apostolate, which was that of good books. His reputation spread and became established. Soon after the departure of Father Virginio and especially after the death of de Diessbach, he would become the unquestioned chief of Catholic resistance against the assaults of incredulity, the traps of rigorism, and the haughty prejudices of anti-Roman regalism.

Works of Charity

There is another kind of apostolic activity, of which we have not yet spoken, which, however, played a great role in Bruno Lanteri's life, as in that of Father de Diessbach, his master—we mean works of charity for the poor, the ill, the infirm, prisoners, all the disinherited of the world.

When we try to rewrite the history of *social Catholicism* in France, we rarely go further back than the foundation by Ozanam of the conferences of St. Vincent de Paul. At most we speak of M. de Melun, or Sister Rosalie, or of the famous "congregation" whose opponents accused it at the time of the Restoration of being primarily a political movement. The history of the *Christian Friendship*, as Bruno Lanteri's life shows it to us, has a whole *social* side, to use today's language. Father de Diessbach had not forgotten that the tradition of the Company of Jesus, from its very beginnings, had required disciples of

St. Ignatius to devote themselves to works of charity, to visiting the poor, caring for the ill in hospitals, exhorting prisoners and so forth. It was while following these holy prescriptions and visiting a hospital that Aloysius Gonzaga, a young novice in the Company, had contracted the plague which was to carry him prematurely to the glory of paradise. As soon as Bruno had fallen under the influence of Father de Diessbach, he had been involved by him in all these works of charity which he pursued unceasingly.

To follow this example, he had only to remember the charity of his father, Dr. Lanteri, which earned him the nickname "father of the poor."

At this period the people had much confidence in their clergy. Father de Diessbach would seek out the wretched, the abandoned or unbelievers wherever they were, in cafes, in slums, in popular meetings. He took his dear Bruno with him everywhere. All his life Father Lanteri would be very assiduous in these works of charity, all the while giving priority to works of spiritual benevolence.

It is indispensable to mention this side of his apostolate here, because for lack of documents we cannot dwell on it at greater length.

Father Lanteri's Prestige

To clarify the influence of Father Bruno Lanteri in the first years of his priesthood, we have two letters from Chambéry dated April 25 and May 14, 1787. These two letters are all the more important in that they are almost our only documents from this period.

We have pointed out above that the bishop of Lausanne, living in Fribourg, had expressed his high esteem of Bruno Lanteri on May 19, 1787. Presumably Father Bruno passed through Chambéry on his way to

Fribourg. He was already known there as an eminent member of the *Clerical Aa*. The *Aa* was directed in principle only to students of theology and to clerics preparing for the priesthood, but former members continued to be respected in the association. The two letters we are going to quote will give us an idea of this respect as far as Bruno Lanteri was concerned. In the first, which comes from a young priest in Chambéry named Louis Tellier, and which was addressed to a priest in the *Aa* in Turin, Sineo della Torre, Lanteri is not named, but since he is named in the second, and the first can only refer to him, there can be no doubt that his stay at Chambéry aroused memorable displays of sympathy and admiration among the *Aa's* members. "...He flashed through like lightning," says Father Louis Tellier regretfully. "I scarcely saw him. I could not contain my inward joy, which was clear to all these pastors, could not moderate my transports at seeing a friend and comrade, such is the strength of the ties which unite us in Jesus Christ. After repeated requests by Canons La Palme, Guillet and Rey, we persuaded him to dine at the seminary. Then, despite the retreat, I went out with him to take him to M. de la Sale, who was so thrilled that he would have liked to detain him for part of the night. I accompanied him to his inn; I left him without hope of seeing him again until he returned. But God arranges things as He wishes.... The next day his work was delayed and he could not leave before noon. Abbot Murgeray, the man who had introduced the *Aa* to Turin a few years before, whom I had informed the day before with this in mind, arranged things so that while he was saying Mass in the cathedral, when he left, without his knowing, he was surrounded by our members. Such were my feelings, if I could have realized them!

"However, I thank the Lord for His generosity towards us: *he revived the dear Aa by his mere presence.*

The salutary advice and the words of consolation which issued from his mouth had a great effect on our hearts. We heard him with pleasure and proposed at least to imitate his zeal in part, if we could not do so in its entirety. Alas! we greatly needed someone to come and see us often, to communicate this spirit of charity to us, this spirit of fervor as we find it among us....

"In that this is the first time that I am honored to write to you, I would not stop yet, if duty did not call me away. But I shall tell you that his journey has been happy so far. Yet he suffered from the excessive cold of Mount Cenis. We were affected by it, too, for some of the vines, etc., are frozen. But his health has not been injured at all. His vision and his intentions are too pure not to draw down on him the graces and blessings of the Lord...."

This almost dithyrambic language is the more extraordinary in that Father Bruno Lanteri was then only 28 years old! In reading such a letter one would say that he was considered a saint. He is surrounded, he is pressed, they want to keep him, to hear him, they rejoice at his fervor, his words stir hearts and warm souls.

But perhaps people will think that the writer of this letter, good Louis Tellier, was particularly inclined to enthusiasm. The second letter, which is also by a Chambéry priest named B. Guillet, is no less warm than the first. It was written to Father de Saint-Georges, a priest and doctor of theology in Turin. It tells us that Turin had written to Chambéry to announce Father Lanteri's journey. This announcement must have been made in such terms that the members of Chambéry's *Aa* were burning with impatience to see him arrive among them.

"His stay, although very brief," writes M. Guillet, "caused remarkable joy. Dear M. Murgeray had the pleasure of seeing his old friend, and the other friends that of knowing a friend hitherto unknown to them. We wanted to hold the *Aa*, and I have no doubt that it was with much satisfaction on both sides. *We saw ourselves what you pointed out as so edifying in dear Lanteri, and it was not hard for us to recognize that the grace of God has borne fruit in him.* One of the greatest satisfactions he gave us was to teach us, thanks be to God, that your *Aa* is continuing its edifying work. I pray the Lord to continue to extend His blessings to you and to give you all a growth in fervor. Dear *Aa* is for us an inexhaustible source of grace, but we shall gather from it only what we work at...."

The rest of the letter shows that if the *Aa* kept up the fervor of a certain number of theology students, there were many others who reacted against it and showed themselves completely "filled with the spirit of the world and subject to their passions."

At Chambéry it was especially in philosophy that evil was spreading among the future priests, and the *Aa* proposed to establish a branch of the association among the philosophers.

The general situation was not bright at this time, two years before the terrible Revolution, which was soon to sweep over Savoy, although Savoy belonged to the Kingdom of Sardinia, not to France.

Let us listen to good M. Guillet on his bitter regrets:

"...I cannot see without groaning," he says, "that in a theology faculty of 50 to 60 students, some of them clerics, the *Aa* has enormous difficulty in finding some who are suitable. But, all are destined to receive Holy Orders, and almost all will be priests in a few years. Alas! I leave you to reflect on and deplore such a state of affairs. The greater the evil, the greater must be our ardor to remedy it.... Let us pray to God fervently that He may deign to look on the needs of His Church and save it from the contempt into which the life of its clerics has cast it...."

Such words are full of instruction for us. It describes or allows us to guess at the deplorable level to which the clergy in Savoy had fallen, at the very least, and in all probability the same was the case, spiritually and morally, in most of the large neighboring country, France. It shows us also the efforts made by a few priests to react against this decadence. We see here in advance the trench which was to be dug a few years later between the two clergies in France, the sworn and the non-sworn or resisters. This same trench would soon exist in Piedmont itself, after the French invasion and under an occupation which was to last sixteen whole years.

To confine ourselves to the purpose of this book, the two letters we have quoted do not leave any room for doubt about the extraordinary influence won within a few years by Father Bruno Lanteri. He had been a priest only five years and already he was considered a leader, a model, an apostle, whose words were received in piety and admiration, and whose mere presence, were it only in passing, during a journey, was enough to reanimate the ardors of the *Aa* group in Chambéry. Truly it would have been difficult to pay such a young priest more resounding or significant honor. As this almost incredible prestige could only have been obtained by numerous achievements, we may justly consider these two letters as a barometric reading of the intense pressure of the apostolic zeal of Bruno Lanteri, of his talents, of his incessant activity, his vigorous personality and his elevated sanctity which everyone recognized in him at that early date!

Bruno Lanteri was to have great need of all his energy and all his virtue to confront the menace of unbelief borne by the revolutionary tide, and supported by the Republic's soldiers!

Now we shall follow him in this new phase of his life.

CHAPTER V

THE SECOND PERIOD OF THE PRIESTLY CAREER OF BRUNO LANTERI, DURING THE FRENCH OCCUPATION (1798-1814)

On April 20, 1792, the legislative assembly had declared war on the Emperor of Austria. The Revolution which until then had appeared peaceful, even passive, suddenly became bellicose and aggressive. Two countries suffered its attacks first: to the north, Belgium, which was an Austrian dependency, and to the southeast, the Sardinian states. The aggressors said that it was a question of waging war on tyrants and delivering the peoples.

In the district of Nice, General Anselme, formerly a noble, attacked the few Sardinian troops, who were unpopular with the inhabitants. Anselme was accompanied by his sister, an "Amazon," who commanded a column of 1,500 cavalry. He took Nice on September 29, 1792, almost without a shot fired, and advanced very quickly to the Alps.

Meanwhile in Savoy another former aristocrat, the ex-Marquis of Montesquiou, had breached the defenses of Montmélian on September 22, two days after the famous battle of Valmy, and entered Chambéry on the twenty-fourth. A few days later the Sardinian troops had evacuated Savoy. The French soldiers were greeted everywhere as liberators. Piedmont could expect attacks in the immediate future. But before the end of the war, both Montesquiou and Anselme were relieved of command as suspect aristocrats, and the former found asylum in Switzerland.

We are sure that these events were followed closely and taken note of by Father Bruno Lanteri. We know how attentive he was to daily events covered by the gazettes, and how carefully he used them to enliven the meetings of the *Christian Friendship* and prepare spirits for what we would call "resistence." Bruno Lanteri at this time was to be the soul of "resistance" in his country not, it appears, of a resistance primarily patriotic and nationalistic, but rather Christian and moral.

What proves that this is not an invention of ours is that among his papers a detailed *"Chronicle history"* has been found, in which all the events and all the acts of the invader are noted very exactly under the two systems of the republican and Gregorian calendars. These annotations span the period from 1789 to 1813.

Bruno Lanteri observed the rising tide of the revolutionary drama, while seeking to erect the most effective barriers against it.

Bonaparte Comes into Play

After the loss of the districts of Nice and of Savoy, the Sardinian Kingdom had a breathing space. The Alps served it as a rampart against new attacks. But in 1796 a young unknown general joined the colors, a Corsican, slender and alert, and at first rated as a mere drawing room general. This was Napoleon Bonaparte. Appointed Commander-in-Chief of the Army of Italy on March 2,

1796, he married Josephine de Beauharnais on the ninth, left Paris on the eleventh, reached Nice on the twenty-sixth and Savona on April 10. His mission was clearly defined by the Directory. It was to push the Austrians out of Italy without delay, without paying attention to the Piedmontese, who would surrender once they were isolated and surrounded. But Bonaparte had his own idea. He was determined to do it his own way. Hurling himself on his adversaries, he won the victories of Montenotte, Millesimo, Dego and Mondovi one after the other.

On April 28 the King of Sardinia signed the armistice of Cherasco, which surrendered to the French Cuneo—Lanteri's hometown—and Tortone. But this armistice was transformed into a peace treaty on May 15, 1796. Vittorio-Amedeo III surrendered six more towns to the French, renounced his claims to Savoy and Nice, and abrogated all alliances with enemies of the Republic. In addition he was to pay about 3 million towards the cost of the war.

All this could not fail to spread terror in Piedmont. What would the victor do? It was known that in France religion had been persecuted, its ministers driven into exile or condemned to the scaffold; it was known that the Republic's soldiers were generally unbelievers, full of mockery of the Catholic faith, and it seemed that the people must expect all kinds of insults, mockeries and blasphemies against religion. But Bonaparte wisely tried to calm people's minds.

On April 26, 1796, he issued the first of his echoingly emphatic pronouncements which were so often to be declaimed in the future:

"Soldiers!" said this proclamation, "in fifteen days you have gained six victories, taken 21 standards, several fortresses, conquered the richest part of Piedmont.... But you have done nothing, for work remains to be done!

Peoples of Italy, the French Army has come to break your chains; the French people are the friend of all peoples: come before her Army with confidence; your property, your religion and your customs will be respected. We wage war generously, and oppose only the tyrants who enslave you."

These were fine promises. It remained to be seen whether they would be kept. Yet it was possible to hope that religious persecution would not be as pronounced nor as bloody as that which had existed in France under the Terror.

Certainly we cannot here go into detail on the military and political fluctuations of the following years. Let us just say that from 1798, and especially after the French victory of Marengo in 1800, the fate of Piedmont was decided for the rest of the Napoleonic era.

For the slender, short General of 1796 had become France's chief of state, first as First Consul, then as Consul for life, finally as Emperor of the French in 1804.

Shortly afterwards he received from the Holy Father the unexpected favor of a coronation in Paris. In him was hailed the man who had ended the Revolution, re-established peace with the Church, negotiated and concluded the Concordat of 1801.

What were to be the consequences of all these events for Piedmont? The country had been purely and simply annexed to the French Empire. Five departments had been hewn out of it: Po, with Turin as its capital; Sesia, with Vercelli as its capital; Stura, with Cuneo as its capital; Marengo, with Alessandria as its capital; and Doria, with Ivrea as its capital. A sixth department, Agogna, with Novara as its capital, was part of the new Kingdom of Italy.

So the Concordat system in force in France after 1802 was to extend to Piedmont. That meant that the Organic Articles, improperly supplemented with regalist provisions by the French Government, were applied in Piedmont as well, and that the famous Four Articles of 1682, containing Gallican principles, were to be taught in seminaries.

Under these circumstances, what was to be the activity of what we have called "the resistance"? Bruno Lanteri was its unquestioned leader. We shall see him in this second period about the most delicate and militant business of his priestly life.

Christian Friendship

Bruno Lanteri must have thanked Providence for arranging things for an action that was both discreet and powerful.

For years he had been considered the real head of the *Christian Friendship*. This association was fundamentally secret. Thus it lent itself unusually well to clandestine action. For "resisters" it represented a first-class weapon. In Bruno Lanteri's hand it was wonderfully effective.

He increased the number of meetings, but took care to hold them in different houses in order to throw an active, suspicious police off the track. His chronicle of events and legislation affecting religion, as we have seen, served as a basis for his exhortations to the "Friends."

In those assemblies the doctrines and deeds of the occupying power were ardently discussed. They studied how to oppose error or violence, and they confirmed one another in knowledge of the truth and in invincible loyalty to Christian unity, whose supreme guardian in the Church is the Pope.

Tracts

In this period Bruno Lanteri stood constantly in the front lines in order to defend Catholic truth. Since he could not print the refutations he wished to oppose the errors of the day, he had copies made by hand by members of the *Christian Friendship*. It would be hard to believe the holy passion which he put at the service of God and of souls through his own and his loyal disciples' work. In the period which concerns us, Bruno composed no fewer than 30 tracts of a polemical character. As soon as they were written, these tracts were passed to copyists, who reproduced them indefatigably to distribute them surreptitiously despite the police. It goes without saying that these tracts were not handed out casually, but were given to families, seminaries, parishes and universities, and that is how they could exercise considerable influence throughout the country.

Let us glance at this literary production, which is Lanteri's main claim to glory as a defender of the faith at such a difficult time!

Here are some titles: *On the oath of fidelity imposed on the clergy; Observations on the new Parisian Catechism, 1806; The true meaning of the name Catholics; Against Napoleon's Organic Articles; The origin of Governments and the origin of the Church; Against Biblical societies; Theological examination of the oath exacted of English Catholics in 1813; Observations on a pretended Concordat* (that of Fontainebleau), etc., etc.

Lanteri did not confine himself to writing. He distributed very widely the best pastoral letters of the bishops of France against the civil constitution of the clergy in 1791, the works of Barruel against the schism which resulted from this constitution, the briefs of Pope Pius VI which condemned it and the bull *Auctorem fidei* by which Pope Pius VI had condemned the Jansenist Synod of Pistoia. To combat Jansenism, which was taught in the seminaries, he distributed a special edition of the works of

Ballerini, on the *Primacy of the Sovereign Pontiff*, and the works of Honore Tournely.

If Lanteri did not take his stand in the nationalist camp and limit himself carefully to the theological domain, it is nonetheless true that patriotic sentiment marched in the same direction and favored his efforts.

Some aspects of his activity must be brought out.

Against Jansenism

Bruno Lanteri was the sworn enemy of Jansenism, as we have seen. He reproached it particularly for disfiguring the idea we must have of God, of our Lord Jesus Christ, of divine compassion, of the gentleness of the divine Son of God, our Savior, of His love for sinners, of His indulgence towards them. But he also blamed them for their opposition to the Pope's authority, the center of Christian unity.

The Jansenists, on their side, reproached Lanteri and his friends for falling into laxity or, as was said in France, "putting cushions under sinners' elbows." They delivered the same reproach, though this is hard to believe, against that fecund, zealous writer who had just died at a very advanced age in the south of Italy, Alphonsus de Liguori.

But Lanteri did not pay any attention to these absurd censures.

"Jansenism," he used to say, "is the open road which leads to Calvinism or unbelief. To the novelties of Jansenism let us oppose Jesus' doctrine of compassion and His example: let us repeat unceasingly: Jesus, our Master, did thus! He said that! *Magister Jesus dixit, Magister Jesus fecit!*"

It was especially during this time of French occupation that he circulated in his work with good books the anti-Jansenist writings of Zaccaria, Bolgeni, Marchetti and Muzzarelli. But principally he used all his resources and all his strength to spread the works of Alphonsus de Liguori. He often returned to them in the meetings of the *Christian Friendship*. He also wrote, in French and Italian, two forceful memoirs: *Reflections on the holiness and doctrine of Msgr. Alphonsus de Liguori,* and *Answer to the question whether Liguori's doctrine is reliable and approved by the Holy See.*

As in other tracts we mentioned above, these two memoirs were copied by hand by the "Friends" and widely distributed among the clergy during the French occupation. They would not be printed until 1825, first at Lyons and later in Milan, Turin, Monza, Ferentino and elsewhere.

It is impossible to calculate the number of copies of the works of St. Alphonsus which were distributed by Lanteri and his people. The work he concentrated on particularly was Liguori's *Homo apostolicus.* We may say that all the partial editions made of this book as of other writings by the saint, between 1790 and 1830, were carried out with the financial help and under the direction of Lanteri and the various groups he ran. Moreover, the great edition of the complete works of the saint published in 1827 by Marietti was very largely funded by Bruno Lanteri.

We can understand why a later disciple of Lanteri could say of him: "In Piedmont he was the defender of sound theology and morality; he was the weightiest hammer against Jansenism."

Against Regalism

But he exerted the very same energy and activity he applied against Jansenism in the struggle against regalism in all its forms. In Napoleon's time, regalism showed itself in the Organic Articles—and we know that Bruno Lan-

Tomb of Father Lanteri in the shrine to the Sacred Heart in Pinerolo, Italy.

teri had refuted them—and in the oath imposed on members of the clergy—we have seen that Lanteri had also written a tract on this oath. Napoleonic regalism again appeared in the *Catechism* of 1806, imposed throughout the Empire, and containing special chapters on obedience owed by all to the all-powerful Emperor. But Bruno Lanteri had not failed to refute this *Catechism* in a tract which was, like the others, copied and distributed widely.

When Napoleon had the gall to try to appoint bishops without the consent of the Pope, whom he had locked up in Savona, and summoned the national council of 1811 to this end, Bruno Lanteri refuted the doctrine of state that the Emperor wished to have triumph, by a well-documented dissertation, where he appealed to the best authors, such as de Marca, Thomassin, Languet and Bossuet. He had this dissertation printed in French, not without great risk to his personal safety, under the title *Of the Primacy of the Roman Pontiff in the confirmation of bishops.*

Naturally this publication was anonymous. It was later ascribed to Muzzarelli, another valiant warrior of the time. Bruno Lanteri knew this and did not claim authorship of the work, out of humility. But the evidence of Craveri, who insists that he saw the manuscript in Lanteri's hand and that he summarized it himself from this manuscript, leaves no doubt about who was the author.

Spiritual Retreats

We must add to all these apostolic labors the profound work Bruno Lanteri accomplished in his numerous spiritual retreats.

No error was more remote from Bruno's mind than what we call activism, which consists in a priest or layman so plunging into external works that he neglects the inward life. For Lanteri it is the inward life, life in union with God, intimacy with Jesus, the good Lord, which comes before everything else. He was particularly devoted, as we shall see in more detail, to the *Spiritual Exercises* following St. Ignatius' method. Not only did he often go on retreat, but he preached the great usefulness of retreats to his friends, to his disciples, to everyone he could reach, and especially to the clergy, young or old. Lanteri considered retreats as "a most potent instrument of divine grace and a certain way for each of us to become a saint and even a great saint."

Very early in his priestly career he had composed a series of sermons on the holy *Exercises* and he continually revised this very personal work which he considered the most important of all. It is remarkable that a man as experienced as Father de Diessbach, himself a Jesuit who was expert in the *Exercises*, recognized and proclaimed as early as 1786, when Lanteri was only 27, his disciple's competence in this regard. He wrote from Vienna to a friend in Turin: "I earnestly exhort you to do the *Exercises* and for that to make arrangements with Lanteri."

It is certain that from 1786 to 1800 Lanteri had already very frequently led retreats in special houses which were then called "factories" which were simply refuges prepared to receive groups on retreat for a few days.

But, under the French occupation, all or nearly all these houses had been closed. Bruno Lanteri decided to establish one which was his personal property and so was protected by the law.

He had a country house, about 12 miles from Turin, called La Grangia. It was a motley collection of buildings which could be adapted to the purpose he had in mind. In 1798 or the years which followed, he made the necessary changes so as to be able to house for a week to a month priests or laymen coming to perform the *Spiritual Exercises*, under his own direction or that of a preacher of his choice.

He managed to arrange things so well that he could gather a score of people on retreat at the same time. This was the ideal number, given his weak lungs and thin voice. Soon La Grangia had a number of devoted regulars. They numbered among them two masters of theology: Rossi and Guala.

It was during these intimate retreats, watched over by God, and in ardent spiritual conferences, that Lanteri healed priestly souls of all the wounds of Jansenism. It was there that he recorded the demagogic follies and abuses of despotic power, and restored minds to the purity of the Gospel and Catholic principles. It is impossible to measure the good done in these meetings. Bruno Lanteri zealously practiced the Gospel's "force them to come in." He had at his disposal in the *Christian Friendship* people we have called "Seekers" who might equally have been called "Recruiters."

And he did not shrink from a certain theatricalism which probably would not be to our taste nowadays, as we shall see. In a villa near La Grangia a man of most scandalous life had died, and his corpse, abandoned by his people, had suffered the ravages of death in a way which well might frighten those who saw it. Bruno thought of having a marble sculpture made reproducing the corpse for use during his retreats. The *Exercises* indeed included meditations on the after-life, which he thought the most effective in a retreat, so he presented this statue to his hearers and instilled a salutary terror in their souls.

But Bruno was not content with La Grangia. Thanks to the concerted efforts of himself and his friend Guala the theologian, he induced the archbishop of Turin,

Msgr. della Torre, to petition the Imperial Government for the reopening of the house and the chapel of St. Ignatius in the Lanzo valley. It was a retreat house, which had existed before the occupation. Permission to reopen it was granted in 1807. Bruno Lanteri and his friend Guala were the first summoned to preach the Exercises there. It is said that at this first retreat there was a government agent who had come deliberately to observe what was thought to be a center of opposition to the Empire. But he was so struck by Bruno's teachings on the holiness and benevolence of the Faith that he converted on the spot and began to lead a completely Christian life.

From everything we have said, it is easy to understand that Bruno Lanteri, when he was later to found a new Congregation, as we shall see, should insist on this Congregation's having as one of its most important apostolic works that of spiritual retreats.

But now we must pass on to the most moving episode in Lanteri's career, the part he played in the pathetic struggle between the Pope and the Emperor.

CHAPTER VI

BETWEEN POPE AND EMPEROR, 1809-1814

The Pope in Savona

It was impossible to interfere with the Pope without wounding Bruno Lanteri to the heart. How great was his grief when he learned, from the gazettes he always read with such care, of the deplorable assault on the person of Pope Pius VII by the Emperor's agents in July 1809.

Conflict had broken out between the Sovereign Pontiff and the short-tempered dominator of Europe about the application of the famous continental blockade. Trouble in Spain and the rupture with Austria in 1809 had forced Napoleon to delay his vengeance. But on May 17, 1809, he signed "in the Imperial camp at Vienna" a decree annexing the Papal States to the French Empire. In the carrying out of this utterly tyrannical decree, the French flag replaced that of the Pontiff over the Castel Sant'Angelo on June 10.

The Pope answered this unjust plundering with the only weapon at his command: excommunication. During the night of June 10-11, the bull of excommunication was posted on the door of several Roman churches, followed on June 11 by "notification" and, on the twelfth by a third document in which Napoleon was identified by name.

Napoleon went into a rage when he was informed. He wrote to Murat on June 20: "I have just received news that the Pope has excommunicated us all. He has excommunicated himself. There will be no more shilly-shallying: he is a raving lunatic and must be locked up."

To carry out his orders, Radet, the chief of police, who had come to Rome on the night of June 12-13, went on the night of July 5-6, 1809, to the Quirinal Palace, where the Pope lived, and had the building silently surrounded. Entering the palace, Radet arrested not only Cardinal Pacca, the Pope's Secretary of State, but the Pope himself, who protested against such an assault. A carriage was waiting. Radet put his two prisoners in it and left for France with them. When he arrived at Grenoble he learned of decisions by the Emperor that the Cardinal should be imprisoned at Fenestrelle in Piedmont while the Pope would be held at Savona.

Only on August 20 did the Pope arrive, after a long and gruelling journey, in Savona. He was housed in the bishop's palace and placed under surveillance by Chabrol, the prefect of the department of Montenotte. The Pope was allowed only a few servants.

The Cardinals who were still in Rome were ordered to move to Paris. Denied his advisers and subjected to captivity, the Pope refused to expedite ecclesiastical business and especially to appoint bishops named by the Imperial Government, as provided for by the Concordat.

The problem of the appointment of bishops thus became the agonizing question of the day.

Bruno Lanteri's Attitude

From one end of the Empire to the other and throughout Christianity, these deeds caused grief and indignation among Catholics. No one was more moved than Bruno Lanteri. He was to use all his energy to minimize the trial imposed on the venerated Pontiff, to fight the regalist doctrines by which Napoleon's government was inspired, and to supply weapons to those who wished to join this theological and political struggle. Bruno Lanteri was a gentle, patient man. But he could not bear a lack of respect for the Head of the Church whom he gladly called: *the sun of Christianity,* or even, *the conductor of the Christian world.*

His first care was to organize an association for the sustenance of the Pope. Napoleon, while depriving him of his States, had given him a pension of 2 million. But Pius VII, justly wounded by this ridiculous alms, refused to accept anything from the hand of the oppressor. He wished to live by support of the faithful alone. His desire was not disappointed. Everywhere committees sprang up to meet his needs. Bruno Lanteri was not the last to gather a group of generous donors. His *Christian Friendship* had never had such an opportunity to show its effectiveness. We see listed in the committee for the benefit of the Holy Father the names of the noblest families in Turin, and among the most intimate friends of Lanteri three distinguished themselves by their eagerness and generosity: Daverio and Guala, who were theologians, and Chèvalier Renato d'Agliano. Some rich members of the middle classes joined them and Gonella, a banker, gave 40,000 francs at one stroke. These sums were taken to the venerated prisoner of Savona by means of a humble porter, whose apparent insignificance put him above or below any suspicion as far as the police were concerned. It is estimated that at least 1 million francs which would be worth $400,000 today, was offered in this way to the Pope.

Chains of Communication

But the prisoner Pope needed things besides material help. What he wanted above all was to be kept in touch

with events so as to be able to lead the struggle against op-
pression, especially to receive the documents essential for
the writings of texts with which he would oppose the
unilateral measures which threatened to submerge the
Church. He had decided not to appoint any more
bishops. By this refusal he caused Napoleon the greatest
difficulty. Religious life was suspended in parishes
without pastors, spirits were disturbed, discontent was
growing on all sides against governmental authori-
tarianism. The Emperor felt this vividly and sought a
way of appointing bishops without the Pope's involvement.

In this struggle of right against might, and truth
against error, it was essential that the Pope should be kept
informed of what was going on outside and should be
provided with the documents indispensable for the refu-
tation of pretensions hostile to his authority.

So there arose, in the midst of Catholic groups, not
only in Turin, around Lanteri and his *Christian Friendship,* but even more in Paris and the cities of France, an
astonishing explosion of devotion and skill. Catholics had
immediately set up secret chains of communication, and
carried them to an almost incredible degree of perfection.
The director-general of the Imperial police in Rome,
Norvins-Montbreton, stated "twenty times" that news
reached these networks from Paris more quickly than
special government couriers. *"I never knew,"* he wrote,
"how the priests managed it!"

We can consider this remark as praise of Bruno Lanteri. He was indeed one of those priests who knew how to
organize secretly networks of correspondence to serve the
good of the Church. These networks began work at once.
They consisted in establishing links between Catholics
who lived all along the road upon which traveled news of
interest to the Church. French historians generally as-
cribe creation of these networks to the mysterious associ-

ation known by the name *Congregation*. We tend to think that all this activity should rather be attributed to the *Christian Friendship*, which we know had spread from Turin to Paris and other towns in France and Italy.

The Pope had not even arrived in Savona when copies of the bull of excommunication against Napoleon were already mysteriously circulating everywhere. Marquis Eugene de Montmorency had the honor of carrying a copy of this bull in his boots from Lyons to Paris. But we know the network ran through the following towns: Savona, Acqui, Mondovi, Turin, Lyons, Paris. Turin was at the center of the chain, and in Turin Lanteri held all the threads.

The "Altar-boys' Cabal"

Napoleon wanted to be kept informed of everything that happened. He was annoyed to sense an active, clever, elusive opposition to his authority. There was a tendency in high places to see in this movement a fad of the young aristocracy. It was called "the altar-boys' cabal." But we know now that among these altar-boys we must number Father Bruno Lanteri, who was no longer young but a good 50 years old. One of the members of a very active part of the network had been identified, a man of 26, Alexis de Noailles. "Who is making fools of youth in this way?" protested Napoleon contemptuously. "Parents have a lot to reproach themselves for."

And he did not understand that, having restored to the papacy its moral prestige, first by negotiating the Concordat and then by the coronation, he was giving it a more radiant halo by his mean persecution of Pius VII. But he limited himself to showing his bad temper by all sorts of measures even meaner-spirited and less worthy of genius: he forbade domestic missions, deleted support for missions abroad from the budget, cancelled the Frays-

sinous Conferences at St. Sulpice, threw young Alexis de
Noailles in prison. And soon we shall see him giving or-
ders to put Bruno Lanteri under house arrest in his villa,
La Grangia!

A Fine Adventure

Before becoming an object of the special attention of
Napoleon's police, Bruno Lanteri had achieved one of the
finest successes of the "altar-boys' cabal."

We have seen that the problem for the Emperor was
that of canonical investiture of bishops. To establish
papal prerogatives on this point, Pius VII needed to have
the text of the Second Council of Lyons, of 1274, which
had solemnly fixed its foundation. But the penalty of
death or deportation threatened anyone who provided
the prisoner of Savona with documents not submitted to
imperial censure. But Bruno Lanteri did not hesitate. He
copied out the Council's decisions, and summoned
Chevalier d'Agliano, whose confessions he heard, and
asked him whether he was willing for love of the Pope
and the Church to face any danger whatever. D'Agliano
enthusiastically declared himself ready to obey. He left
for Savona, was granted audience by the Pope, and,
while kissing the Pontiff's feet, furtively slipped the
needed document into the folds of his cassock. The Pope
used it to write his famous letters to Cardinals Caprara
and Maury, Bishop Osmond and the capitular vicar of
Paris, d'Astros. These letters, forwarded by the network,
were immediately distributed to the people. The imperial
government had been outwitted. Napoleon had a fit of
rage. For him it was as if he had lost a battle. He spoke of
having d'Astros shot, then was satisfied with imprisoning
him in Vincennes, along with Cardinals di Pietro, Gabri-
elli and Opizzoni, who were best known for their loyalty
to the Pope.

He also ordered his police to search everywhere for the links in the mysterious "chain." It was impossible for Lanteri not to be in the first rank of suspects. Indeed he had never stopped writing tracts, as we have said, and having them recopied by hand, by his friends, to distribute them to the public. He had just finished writing one of his vigorous expositions against Napoleon's plan to summon a national council in Paris to decide the irritating question of canonical investiture of bishops.

On January 29, 1811, the imperial police made an unexpected descent on Father Lanteri's house. The police searched thoroughly every corner of the dwelling. Lanteri watched their search, a smile on his lips. He had already had faithful Father Loggero as his secretary for some time. Loggero had taken care to remove all suspicious papers. The search revealed nothing. Father Lanteri thought that from then on he would be safe, and resolved to continue his activities, although more cautiously than in the past. But soon he realized that the danger was not over for him.

The Chain Discovered

Ten days after the search we just described, the Duke of Rovigo (Savary), the internal security minister in Paris, wrote to the chief of police in Turin:

"Sir, I have just had Mr. Bertaut du Coin of Lyons arrested. This man travelled to Savona last November, in the vicinity of the Pope, dispatched by several factious, trouble-making priests. He saw the Pope, delivered and received messages, and returned to Lyons, where he has been arrested. He admits the fact and purpose of the journey, but refuses to explain the means or the intermediaries of this correspondence. But I found in his papers an article of which I send you a copy. I have no doubt that these are the principal agents at different points of the line from Savona to Turin...."

After the arrest of Bertaut du Coin, Bruno Lanteri knew that his freedom was at stake. The police wanted to know if this line of communication had already functioned and how secret communications were transmitted between the prisoner Pope and Paris. The minister ordered the arrest of all whose replies to interrogation should appear suspect and insincere. The names in Bertaut du Coin's papers were the Chevalier d'Agliano, Father Bruno Lanteri, Father Daverio, Demetrius Cordero de Montezemolo, Mondovi, M. de Sinsan and M. Conradi, a Turin engineer.

The reply of d'Auzers, chief of police in Turin, is dated January 29.

This was the day of the search we discussed above. The chief of police gives fairly full information about Father Bruno Lanteri. He states that he has had him questioned most carefully. Here are the most striking parts of his report on this subject:

"This priest," he writes, "who is considered a very pious and very honest man here, was pointed out to me by a secret agent as not being very favorable to the government, especially since the troubles with the Pope. But since he is extremely careful in his remarks and in his activities, I had found no proof, but had him secretly under surveillance."

So Lanteri was suspected, but there was no precise complaint against him. There is a section of the report which interests us greatly. Without being named, the *Christian Friendship* is referred to. What did the police know about it? This is what the Turin police chief now tells us:

"I had discovered," he writes, "that in Turin there *used to be,* that is before the French occupied the country, *a kind of association of Jesuit priests and clerics after*

*the Jesuits were suppressed. These associates were to keep
secret, even from their confessors, what was discussed or
decided in these meetings.*

"Father Lanteri was the head of this group, which
still corresponded with Vienna, Austria, eight years ago
[i.e., in 1803] through a Piedmontese priest named
Virginio who had lived in that city for 10 years, but died
some three years ago [in fact he had been dead six years].

"It also corresponded with Paris, through another
Piedmontese priest long established in that city, Father
Sinico. He had to return to Rome a few years ago: I do
not know what has become of him since then, for he has
not been back to Piedmont. This society was small and
apears to have ceased its correspondence some time
ago."

As we can see, the police knew that the *Christian
Friendship* existed, but knew almost nothing of what it
did. They saw in it a kind of offshoot of the Company of
Jesus, after it was suppressed.

Next the report speaks of the interrogation of Father
Lanteri. This interrogation produced little. Lanteri admitted that he had seen Mr. Bertaut du Coin once or
twice, "when he came to confession." But, since he had
been ill, he could not even remember if he had heard his
confession or not, and certainly he had not given him any
instructions for Savona. During the search of January 29,
the only thing that had been found was a copy of the bull
excommunicating the Emperor, dated June 10, 1809.

But d'Auzers' conclusion is to be remembered:

"I cannot conceal," he said, "that Father Lanteri is
very influential here, through confessions. *He is one of
the most sought-out confessors in the city.* Although his
health has been poor for some months, which forces him
to stay in his bedroom, *many individuals, even in the influential class, have kept him as their spiritual director.*"

As a measure of administrative repression, d'Auzers proposed that an order should be issued to the archbishop of Turin to remove from Father Lanteri his power to hear confessions, and that he should be banished, either to Cuneo, his birthplace, or to a country house he had near Turin, since the weakness of his health would not permit him to be moved far.

Similar measures were recommended for Father Daverio, who was identified as sharing "the exaggerated opinions concerning religion of his friend Father Lanteri," and as a "former member of the same society for maintaining Jesuit moral principles."

The proposals were indeed carried out shortly afterwards against the two friends. On February 27, 1811, the minister reported to the Emperor. On March 9 the minister for religions, Count Bigot de Préameneu, wrote to Msgr. della Torre, archbishop of Turin, to have Lanteri's and Daverio's power to hear confessions suspended because of their "pronounced fanaticism." On March 21 the archbishop, announcing to the minister for religions that his orders had been put into effect and that Father Lanteri had left for his country house, defended Lanteri with some courage. He insisted that Father Lanteri knew no one in Savona, that he had been in such poor health for the past year and a half that he had scarcely written to anyone, aside from a half-dozen business letters for his family, and that it was very unjust for him to be denounced as an "extreme fanatic."

"Everyone who knows him," the archbishop wrote plainly, "can swear to the fact that not only has he never had anything to do with politics but that throughout his life he has abstained from social activities. *On the contrary, his character tends to solitude, he is very withdrawn, a man of few words, and consequently has been without mundane involvements.*

"If he has been accused of hearing many confessions, he has done so only in strict accordance with canon law, and what drew people to him for confessions was that he knew French very well and could hear confession in that tongue. Recently his poor health had prevented him from hearing confession in church. As a result he could hear confession only at home, and even then only rarely."

The archbishop identifies another important characteristic for us when he says that he is "normally active only in visiting invalids." Father Lanteri was devoted, as we have said, to works of charity. He spent his time hearing confession and helping the sick! The archbishop also reported very favorably on Father Daverio. He concluded by begging permission for Father Lanteri to spend two weeks in Turin, after Easter, for his "private affairs" and for medical treatment.

Lanteri Imprisoned in La Grangia

On March 25, 1811, Lanteri had gone to his country house, La Grangia, which we know already. He was readily granted permission to return for two weeks to Turin after Easter. He even received an extension. But apart from these few weeks at the beginning, he was to remain imprisoned and under surveillance at La Grangia until the fall of the Empire, in other words for three years, from 1811 to 1814.

Without bothering in the least about the things done to him, he saw in them a sign of divine mercy. For him these three years were a time of almost complete solitude, rest, prayer and contemplation. It must have seemed to him that God wanted him to fulfill his original vocation as a Carthusian. He knew how to get in touch with the Sovereign Pontiff, and he used the "chain" which the police had failed to destroy completely to ask and receive His Holiness' oral permission to keep the Holy Sacrament in his private chapel. From then on he could devote himself to It to his heart's content. He spent the bulk of his time at the feet of the Prisoner of love in the tabernacle. He was later to say that the day on which he had been granted so great a favor—by verbal authorization of the Pontiff, transmitted by the archbishop of Turin—had been "one of the most beautiful of my life." From then on, the "house arrest" to which he was subjected seemed to him as sweet as it was advantageous.

As he had always been the friend of good books, he had to have at La Grangia his favorite authors: Holy Scripture, St. Thomas Aquinas, St. Bonaventure. He wrote thirty pamphlets on the Eucharist, on God's perfection, and on degrees of perfection. His friend, Canon Craveri, wrote: "During his years at La Grangia, he meditated deeply on divine things, with the help of the works of the seraphic doctor—St. Bonaventure—and found such delight and enlightenment in them that he said that he had never known God so well until he read these pious works. I cannot doubt that his soul then attained the highest levels of contemplation."

Forced residence at La Grangia also aided his health. He went there with some apprehension. His sight had deteriorated so far that he could no longer work without a secretary, his stomach was sometimes so disturbed that he felt his life endangered. He could not heal completely at La Grangia, but he recovered enough physical vigor and morale while there to resume his studies and his apostolate as a preacher of retreats, to a degree which astonished everyone who knew him.

For the Pope, No Matter What

We should not imagine for a moment that Bruno Lanteri had let himself be intimidated by the Emperor's rages or the threats of the police. At La Grangia, which was fairly isolated, a dozen miles from Turin, as we have said, and with poor road links to the parish, he escaped the searching eyes of the government's agents. So he could receive many visitors. He could lodge them either to conduct them through the *Exercises* or to discuss current events. On leaving this oasis of holiness, his friends would return to Turin and elsewhere more than ever devoted to the service of God and His earthly Vicar.

But he did not stop there. Since the police had been unable to clarify the mystery of the tracts which were circulating surreptitiously in Turin, he wrote all the more, and had them copied as before by his disciples for secret distribution. Letters, exhortations, short polemics—he neglected nothing that could stir up his friends' zeal.

During his "exile"—as his banishment from Turin was called—his most important tract was *On a so-called Concordat.* This dealt with the agreement Napoleon extorted from the Pope at Fontainebleau where the Pontiff, who was already exhausted from his imprisonment in Savona, had been transferred. Bruno Lanteri had no trouble demonstrating that the articles of this so-called Concordat were simply an unforgivable extortion by the Emperor in desperation, for they completely contradicted the Pope's record. Thus it was not the Pope speaking in this document, but the perfidy of Napoleon and his agents.

"Let the Holy Father speak freely," Lanteri concluded, "and everyone will see how closely his voice always conforms with the divine institution of the Church. But that is exactly what they are afraid of! That is why the Holy Father is not left at liberty!"

We know that the Pope was no sooner delivered from his abject servitude than he made it his first task to deny everything he had been forced to sign and to declare the Concordat at issue null and void.

Was this paper by Lanteri seized by the police? Or did some hint of something reach official circles? We do not know. But it seems likely that the authorities had been alerted, for one day when Father Lanteri was quietly engrossed in his ordinary studies at La Grangia the Turin police came once more to search his home.

Perhaps Father Lanteri trembled inwardly on this occasion. The manuscript of his tract on the spurious Concordat was indeed there. Had faithful Loggero taken care to suppress every trace of the offense? Father Lanteri used to place his intimate papers in the lower part of a prayer stool which is preserved as an object of veneration in the Oblates' house of the Sacred Heart in Pignerolo. And the manuscript was there in this humble hiding-place. Simply lifting the board of the kneeler would disclose it. We suppose that the good priest silently made a fervent prayer: *"Thy will be done!"* God's will was that the secret should not be discovered. The policemen searched everywhere, found nothing, and, seeing that their hunt was futile, went away after apologizing for the disturbance caused by their visit!

All this took place towards the end of the Empire. The hour had struck when Napoleon would have something very different to do than persecute an unarmed old Pope. No doubt he realized inwardly that of all the errors he might have committed in his resplendent career, this was the most regrettable and ultimately the most disastrous for himself. It has often been said that he had boasted that the Pope's excommunications would not strike his soldiers' guns from their hands. If he really did say this, it would merely prove that nature had omitted prophecy from the talents with which it endowed the impulsive Corsican. He had long believed in the star of his destiny. But it was setting. A page was about to be turned. While the Pope would go back to Rome, the Emperor would go into exile in his turn, and a day would come when his closest relatives would find no safer refuge than the Papal States to which the Pope was restored!

CHAPTER VII

THE THIRD PERIOD
IN THE SACERDOTAL
CAREER OF
BRUNO LANTERI
1814-1830

The Ebb

The month of April 1814, was Napoleon's ebb-tide. On April 20, Napoleon left for the isle of Elba. Three days before, he had signed his abdication at Fontainebleau. Immediately there was a series of princely journeys, from one end of Europe to the other, as the old sovereigns were restored. In France, Louis XVIII was to date documents from the nineteenth year of his reign, as if the Empire and even the Revolution had been only a dream. On May 20, 1814, the city of Turin acclaimed its King Vittorio-Emanuele I, who had been absent in Sardinia with all his family since 1799.

On May 24, Pius VII returned to Rome to endless applause. Everywhere prison gates were opened. Everywhere the victims of tyranny regained their liberty. Bruno Lanteri accordingly left La Grangia to take up his work in Turin with new energy and, thanks to God, restored health.

He had conducted his struggle courageously, but it is plain that the organizations he had run had suffered more or less under the dramatic circumstances we have outlined. His *Christian Friendship*, his dear *Clerics' Aa*, had undoubtedly borne fruit, and their members were the people who had provided Bruno Lanteri with the most precious cooperation in the memorable battles he had waged. But the meetings had been suspended. It was known that the police had pierced the secrecy of the *Christian Friendship*. Besides, conditions had changed. Many changes were necessary. While beginning work again at the foundations, by recruiting new members to replace the old, who were either dead or dispersed, Bruno Lanteri realized that he could no longer limit himself by rules formulated in another era. It is strange to notice that at the very moment when secret societies called Carbonari were to multiply in Italy, but with a most hostile attitude to religion, Bruno Lanteri discarded secrecy for the Catholic organizations he dreamed of restoring. When he was young, Father de Diessbach had given him as the mark of his complete confidence the *cipher* in which all the *Christian Friendship* correspondence was written. There had been something similar in the *Aa*. Father de Diessbach had added a third group, the *Sacerdotal Friendship*, in 1782, of which Bruno Lanteri had immediately become the most active member. But this Friendship was to remain secret too. The *Sacerdotal Friendship*, deeply rooted in Turin, had spread less readily than the *Christian Friendship* to other Italian or foreign towns.

We can nevertheless trace the existence of the *Sacerdotal Friendship* from 1782 to 1811. But the departure of Father Lanteri for La Grangia by order of the police in 1811 had been its coup de grace.

Restoration of Sacerdotal Friendship

Before even thinking of the *Christian Friendship*, although it had been so prominent in his life and heart,

Father Lanteri judged that the most pressing need was to regroup priests. So he set out to restore the *Sacerdotal Friendship*. The membership was not limited, as had been necessary when it was a secret society. We soon learn that the *Friendship* involved about 60 priests. Among them we can identify experienced veterans like the theologians Daverio, who had shared Lanteri's trials, Guala and Rossi, Father Andreas, Father Loggero, but also a constellation of young priests, eager to perfect themselves, under Bruno's direction, in the study of theology, in the practice of personal interior life and in all the methods of apostolate. The members of the *Friendship* were to devote themselves particularly to popular religious instruction, not only in parishes, but in hospitals and prisons. They were to give the *Spiritual Exercises* to which we know Father Lanteri attached such great importance. And they were to unite works of temporal charity, by visiting the poor where they lived, to works of spiritual charity. To this end there would be groups of three or four *Friends*, directed by an experienced, pious priest, who would exercise their zeal in the various areas just specified. The most common scenes for their magnificent activity were the churches of St. Francis, St. Teresa and St. Dalmatius; St. John's and the maternity hospitals and the military hospital; the Senatorial, Forced Labor and medium-term prisons.

We cannot omit the sweet and loving figure of St. Joseph Cafasso, who had just been born at Castelnuovo d'Asti on January 16, 1811, and who, in Turin shortly after Father Lanteri's death, was to exercise such a moving ministry in theological teaching, spiritual direction and charity for prisoners and those condemned to death. The line from Lanteri to Cafasso runs directly through Luigi Guala, and we know that his line runs on through to that admirable saint, John Bosco. It is surely one of the most certain and eminent of Bruno Lanteri's claims to glory that he prepared such harvests as these two names, so illustrious in the history of Christian charity and social action.

Without Lanteri, without his *Sacerdotal Friendship*, without the intensive action of his exhortations and example, it is overwhelmingly probable that we would have had neither Joseph Cafasso nor Don Bosco!

We should point out that in December 1815 the *Sacerdotal Friendship* in Turin, directed by Father Lanteri, sought out and was granted affiliation with the *Pious Union of St. Paul*, founded in Rome around 1790 by members of the clergy. After this affiliation the Turin *Friendship* took the name *Pious Union of St. Paul* of Turin in the official records of its meetings.

The *Christian Friendship*

But Bruno Lanteri did not forget the Catholic lay world. Along with the *Sacerdotal Friendship* he planned to relaunch the *Christian Friendship*, which he had received from Father de Diessbach and which had played so fruitful a role in the years of tempest. The temporary absence of some of the old influential members forced him to wait until 1817 to breathe life into the association.

The first meeting of the *Christian Friends* took place at the palace of Marquis Caesar d'Azeglio on March 3, 1817.

At this first meeting, presided over by Father Lanteri, all the members present agreed that the "absolute secrecy" which had been observed until then was no longer right for the times. There was no question any more of hiding and obscuring what was going on, the time of the catacombs was over. On the contrary, the moment had come to live and work in daylight. If unbelief was more than ever at work in the shadows, if secret societies were multiplying to spread the spirit of revolution and hatred for the clergy, it was important to give the *Christian Friendship* an open, commanding face, to avoid all confusion with suspect groups which fled the clarity of daylight.

But it was good that the *Christian Friendship*, which had survived the time of trial, should keep its proven framework and useful regulations. So it was decided that a new society would be created, modeled after the *Christian Friendship* and to some extent under its patronage and direction, but to be made up only of laypeople and to do all its work in the public arena, with statutes known to all and without any obligation to use ciphers or to meet secretly. This new *Christian Friendship* would, however, depend on the old, in the sense that it would derive its impetus from the old, that its catalogue of good books would be the same and would not admit new books without the approval of the priests in charge of the latter.

Let us examine this closely: what is this new form of *Christian Friendship*, which we have seen at work since the time of Father de Diessbach? It is in truth exactly what we now call *Catholic Action*. And if we have stressed the amazing fertility of Father Lanteri's *Sacerdotal Friendship*, pointing out that without it there would have been neither Joseph Cafasso nor John Bosco, we must now say that it is again Bruno Lanteri's name that is to be found at the source of Catholic Action in Italy.

We need only review the names of the most remarkable members of the *Christian Friendship*, as just defined, to bow in admiration before his influence and the abundance of his fruits.

We must place Marquis d'Azeglio in the first rank of *Christian Friends*. His palace was its base, and became its first headquarters. Around him we find the most distinguished names of Piedmontese aristocracy: Marquis Giuseppe Massimino, Secretary of the Treasury; Count Luigi Gattinara, regent of the Chancellery of State; Count

Piobesi di Guarene; the Chevaliers Borghese, Luigi di Collegno and Ferrario di Castelnuovo.

Catholic Friendship

A new member, the most prestigious of all, joined in November 1817. Who was this figure, around whom stirred murmurs of admiration? It was that great writer, Joseph de Maistre, one of the great thinkers of his time, the profound and captivating author of *Evenings in St. Petersburg* and of so many works whose titles are known to every scholar.

It was thanks to him that the *Christian Friendship* changed its name and became the *Catholic Friendship*. He it was who proposed this title, which was finally adopted after some discussion and hesitation.

We must note that it was in the atmosphere of the *Catholic Friendship* that he published in 1819, his beautiful book *On the Pope*, in which the spirit prevailing in the association is dazzlingly clear. Two years later, shortly before his death, he published his book *On the Gallican church*. When he died, his son Rodolphe de Maistre replaced him in the *Catholic Friendship*. Many other names which were the brightest in Piedmontese society could be listed with his. But the activity of the *Friendship* was not confined to Turin. It corresponded widely. The "Friends" divided this task among themselves: Senator Chevalier de Castelnuovo, for example, corresponded with Alessandria, Acqui, Carmagnole, Casale; his colleague Luigi de Collegno with Geneva and Pinerolo; Chevalier Pallavicino with Ivrea and Saluces; Chevalier Borghese with Biella; Count Tornielli with Novara, and Marquis d'Azeglio, the principal mover of all this work, with Rome, France and America. Among the people to whom they sent their messages were figures as eminent as Msgr. Lambruschini, Archbishop of

Genoa, Msgr. d'Angennes, Bishop of Alessandria, and Msgr. Bigex, Bishop of Pinerolo.

The essential aim of the *Friendship* was to combat the poisonous influence of bad books and newspapers, to spread a good press, as *Christian Friendship* had since its foundation by Father de Diessbach. Thus it was simply an extension of the latter. It had borrowed its catalogue, it received its first library funds and resources from it. But it very quickly added its own efforts: generally books or short but substantial and effective tracts. It also distributed little books of a popular kind, with such titles as: *Think about it!—The human heart's return to God —Thoughts on the errors of our day—The book of the warrior.* It also circulated more impressive books, like those of Gerdil, Marchetti, Ballerini, Pallavicini, and Lamennais' *Essay on Indifference.* We should not neglect to mention that they also combatted the action of Protestant Bible societies, by spreading Catholic editions of the Bible and especially of the New Testament.

Some numbers will give an idea of this activity: according to the records of the *Friendship,* the number of books distributed directly by the *"Friends"* rose in 1820 to 13,070; in 1821, to 21,268; in 1822 it was 20,110. To these figures we must add works distributed by preachers of missions in parishes. The missions of the Oblates alone, about whom we shall speak later, distributed 18,347 volumes between 1823 and 1825 at the *Friendship's* expense.

In 1825 Marquis Caesar d'Azeglio, replying to calumnies against the *Friendship,* could sum up the association's balance sheet in these terms:

"In the eight years of the *Friendship's* existence, hundreds of thousands of volumes have been distributed, more than 10,000 of which have been sent to America."

The high costs of this beneficial propaganda were met by private subscription. But the King himself, Carlo-

Felice, glorying in the first years of his reign in the title
First Catholic Friend, each year gave generously to the
work.

Experiment with a Catholic Newspaper

It was in line with this ardent activity that the first
Catholic newspaper was established, in an admittedly
modest form but still worthy of the respect owed an an-
cestor. *The Friend of Italy* appeared for the first time in
1822, in a small format, appearing at first once a month
in 50-page fascicles. A periodical of this kind would today
be called a journal rather than a newspaper. But *The
Friend of Italy* nonetheless played a fine role in Italy
among the periodicals of the period. Its founding editor
and almost sole writer was Marquis Caesar d'Azeglio,
whom we have seen heading the *Catholic Friendship* and
who was always in the thick of the fray.

He must be seen as a faithful disciple of Bruno Lanteri. A man of deep faith, of an elevated Christian life,
cultured, he had matured for decades in Lanteri's school.
He had always been one of the most active and devoted
participants in the *Christian Friendship*. In accepting the
direction of the youthful *Catholic Friendship* he remained true to his past. It has been said that a single man
of this caliber suffices to glorify Bruno Lanteri, who was
his master, his model, his counsellor, his father.

Before founding his *Friends of Italy*, Caesar
d'Azeglio, who had voluntarily exiled himself to Florence
during the first years of the French occupation of Piedmont, had brought to birth a publication of the same
type, appearing once a month, under the title *The Bee*.
The "Christian Friends" in Florence, linked since their
foundation with the *Christian Friendship* in Turin,
called it the *Gazette*. This sort of Catholic review survived—even after the return of d'Azeglio to Turin in

1806—until 1816. *The Bee* and the *Friend of Italy*, are, with the *"Voice of Truth"* which appeared in Modena, the oldest Italian Catholic journals known to us. When we think of the colossal strength of the adversaries of the Catholic faith at that time, although they marched under different banners—Jansenist, regalist, liberal, Voltairean —we can only admire the courage and faith of these champions of Catholic truth and of loyalty to the Pope and the Church. The intensity of the battle is shown by the reaction which took place in 1827 in the mind of King Carlo-Felice which led to the suppression of the *Catholic Friendship.* We have said that the King, a good Christian in private, liked to call himself the First Catholic Friend and had contributed generously to the work from the beginning. But the movement's adversaries, recruited as we just said from a variety of sectors of the public, committed themselves to constant attacks on the King's mind. The most childish calumnies circulated in the liberal press and in the salons. The *Catholic Friendship* was represented as a sequel to "the Jesuit party"—rather in the same way as in France at that time there were attacks on the "priestly party" and the revival of Jesuitism. If we were to believe the attackers, this was a "dangerous sect" which planned to establish domination over States, subject Governments to itself and humble all secular authority before Papal omnipotence. At first Carlo-Felice did not let himself be influenced by these perfidious and absurd insinuations. But he was unstable in character and was surrounded by ministers imbued with regalism. They managed to persuade him that the true interest of his crown required suppression of the *Catholic Friendship.* On the pretext of ending all societies, secret or not, he forbade the meetings of the *Friendship*, which was dissolved in the spring of 1827 after ten years of glorious activity.

Even in the first years of Carlo-Alberto, who succeeded Carlo-Felice in 1831, it was still commonplace to denounce the supposed "Jesuit influence" and to speak of the misdeeds of the dissolved *Catholic Friendship*.

These lunatic allegations are to us a sign of homage to Bruno Lanteri's apostolate. It is obvious that he must be considered the father of Italian Catholic Action.

Now we shall see him founding a new Congregation: the *Oblates of the Virgin Mary*.

CHAPTER VIII

THE OBLATES
OF THE
VIRGIN MARY

A Beautiful Initiative

The idea of the Oblates did not come first from Bruno Lanteri. But he was so visibly the leader of all sacerdotal action in the Sardinian Kingdom, that he was almost at once asked for his advice and instructions.

At Carignano, a small town a few miles from Turin from which the ruling dynasty, Savoy-Carignano, took its name, three zealous priests, Father Giovanni Reynaudi, Father Antonio Biancotti and Father Agostino Golzio, had decided to join like brothers to work together for their personal sanctification and the salvation of souls, by fighting the ravages left by the French Revolution and the Napoleonic occupation. This was in 1815, after what is called the "Restoration."

In the minds of these pious companions, three methods would work towards their objective:

1. the ministry of preaching and confession; 2. the creation of a school to mold young children for the priesthood to carry on the torch from the old; 3. the assiduous practice of help for the poor.

Certainly they would have been very surprised if they had been told that they were going to found a new Congregation!

They needed a center—a church and a house—to pursue their objective.

They had both. Father Agostino Golzio had been rector of the church and convent of St. Mary of Graces in Carignano since 1808. The house had belonged to the Augustinians. Like other religious Orders, they had been suppressed in 1800. The church and the house were almost in ruins, and proposals were made to demolish them and build a square and a market.

Reynaudi and his companions sought the King's permission, as required by law, to use the building for their plans. It seemed they would succeed, but then they met such a furious opposition that they had to give up any hope in this direction. Reynaudi went to Rome and tried to enter the Company of Jesus. But having failed in this because of his poor sight, he went back to Carignano, very discouraged but resolved to do his best to achieve his salvation and that of his fellows. At that moment the favor they no longer dared to hope for was granted them. A royal decree gave them title to St. Mary of Graces. This happy news stunned them all, the more so in that news of the concession coincided with Reynaudi's return, which they wished for but did not expect. Golzio and Biancotti begged him to direct the projected work once more. He hesitated at first, wishing to reflect, and made a fervent retreat to seek divine enlightenment. Finally he made a decision. It was agreed that they would meet at his house until the royal decree took effect. A young priest named Carlo Aicardi had joined Golzio and Biancotti. They decided to undertake a shared schedule, to spend an hour a day in meditation, to do half an hour of pious reading, to have a spiritual conference, and to make an examination of conscience every evening. Without taking vows, they intended to live as if they had.

Reynaudi, who was always cautious and modest, sought advice everywhere to ensure the proper direction of the swelling burden placed on his shoulders. He sought advice of theologian Luigi Guala, among others, and offered him leadership of the new group, but Guala humbly refused the offer and suggested he should ask his master Bruno Lanteri, who was, he said, the man best able to enlighten Reynaudi.

Lanteri was then at his country house. That was where he received one day a visit from Reynaudi. As was his custom, he greeted him most kindly. They discussed the advantages and disadvantages of the project at length. He kept Reynaudi at La Grangia for several days, and asked him to make a retreat to consult the Lord. Reynaudi eagerly agreed. Day by day, Lanteri told his guest his inspirations. Neither of them could doubt that these inspirations came from God Himself.

Lanteri urged on his guest the great effectiveness of the Spiritual Exercises and the necessity of popular missions to parishes, in order to revive that awareness of Christianity which had been so diminished and weakened by unhappy circumstances. He spoke to him of the errors of the day, of the urgency of combatting them, and hence of knowing them first. To do this it was necessary to form an educated, young, active clergy, devoted to the Church and the Holy See, resolved to struggle against the bad press and to propagate good reading matter.

Lanteri, as we know, was inexhaustible on this theme. He expressed the dominant passion of his priestly life in these ardent words to Reynaudi. Of course, the latter was convinced of this already. With profound joy he saw his own apostolic ambitions defined, his first ideas expanded, and a project for a new apostolic society set up, destined undoubtedly to reap the most abundant harvests.

But, his confidence in himself shrinking, he begged Father Lanteri to take direction of the work whose program and outlines he had sketched so well. Bruno hesitated in his turn. He gave his guest only a vague hope. Urged once more, he said he wanted to consult the Lord at greater length, and also to know if the scheme he had drafted for Reynaudi would be accepted by his companions. He also objected that he could not immediately desert the works he had underway in Turin.

The Project Takes Shape

Reynaudi had nothing more pressing to do when he got back to Carignano than to report everything to his companions. He did it with such warmth that they all agreed that Father Lanteri's plans must be adopted, and that he must be asked to put them into effect himself. From that day Lanteri was, in all their hearts, the real head of the nascent institute.

They went back to find him. They told him their unanimous wish. He let himself be persuaded and rapidly wrote some short, precise rules which ended in this magnificent formula: *Lex sit amor, directrix oboedientia:* Let love be the law and obedience the guide.

But it had become clear to all of them that they were going to found a congregation. For that they needed canonical approval first. The see of Turin was vacant, so they addressed Msgr. Emmanuel Gonetti, the capitular vicar.

This prelate knew the petitioners' zeal and high virtue so well that he issued without delay the decree of approval which was requested. The name chosen for the institute was *Congregation of the Oblates of the Virgin Mary.*

He did even more: since the royal decree bestowing St. Mary of Graces on the companions had not yet been carried out, because of the opposition of the pastor of Carignano, he ordered the latter, in his capacity as royal sub-bursar, to install the henceforth canonically established society in possession of the house and the church.

This was done on November 13, 1816.

The transfer took place, with a joy we can imagine, on the eve of the Feast of the Immaculate Conception. Mary herself seemed to welcome her sons into the sanctuary restored to receive them.

First Harvests

We have spoken of "abundant harvests." They were seen at once. Bruno Lanteri and Reynaudi decided first of all to preach the *Spiritual Exercises* at Carignano itself. The preachers chosen were two intimate friends of Bruno, his devoted secretary Giuseppe Loggero and Father Antonio Lanteri. The success was immediate and immense. In a memorandum in his own hand, Reynaudi has described the confessionals besieged by the crowd of the faithful, the church always filled to capacity, the Oblates transported with joy. The most hardened sinners, the most obstinate atheists, were converted. Many of them, after 30 or 40 years of resisting grace, became apostles in their turn restoring their fellow sinners to the Faith.

Since Lanteri could not, as he had warned them, give up instantly his works in Turin, whose character and importance we know, he had Reynaudi act as his deputy. Reynaudi deserved all the confidence placed in his zeal and skill. The most astounding conversions continued to take place. Let us note at once that Reynaudi would continue his ministry as a preacher for a long time. For 20 years he was to tour the towns and villages of Piedmont. He would preach 300 missions and at his death would leave a very important legacy to the young society, which he had started and of which he was one of the glories. His ashes rest at the foot of the high altar in Turin's Consolata.

The Turin Residence

Besides his *Sacerdotal Friendship* and *Christian Friendship*, which kept Father Lanteri in Turin a while longer, there was the delicate issue of establishing an ecclesiastical residence, about which he had thought for a long time. We know what this meant. The reader will not have forgotten that Bruno Lanteri had had to prepare for three years for a pastoral examination, after his ordination as a priest, before he could hear confessions. This preparation was required of all young priests. They were no longer in the seminary, but had to seek rooms with families or in hotels, while they pursued such important studies. Bruno Lanteri had seen too much of the inconveniences of this practice, and had too great a sense of priestly holiness not to seek a remedy for this situation. In his *Sacerdotal Friendship* he had tried to group young people by putting them in the benevolent care of their elders. But a concrete organization to match the measures he had taken was lacking. He had the idea of creating a residence. Today we would call it a student dormitory. Nowadays all Catholic universities have such residences. So do secular universities, except that they pay more attention to material facilities for the students than to the creation of a morally healthy atmosphere for their spiritual development.

With the foundation of the new congregation of Oblates, Bruno Lanteri thought the time ripe to create the student residence for young priests which was so sorely lacking in Turin. Towards the end of 1816, he presented a long petition to Msgr. Gonetti, the capitular vicar, to allow the extension to Turin of the congregation of

Oblates in Carignano. He listed the following objectives for the congregation in Turin: the preaching of the Exercises; the ministry of souls in the confessional; the apostolate of charity in hospitals and prisons; and "a residence for new priests and public teaching, when this is considered opportune."

The petition explained clearly and at length the advantages of such an establishment. It listed the problems that must be solved: its quarters, its means of support, the subjects that should be included in the work. It proposed the Franciscan monastery as the location, from which the brothers had been hounded during the occupation, on condition that compensation was paid the religious who retained the title.

Father Lanteri also wisely foresaw objections and answered in advance.

The capitular vicar welcomed the proposal warmly. But the Oblates needed government approval. The regalists who were on watch in all the state's ministries were normally very hostile to congregations and little disposed to favor the spread of a new one. Nonetheless, Bruno Lanteri filed his request for permission with the royal treasury early in 1817. Then he waited. He had to wait a long time. In the following summer, when nothing had been done, he renewed his request. This time there was a glimmer of success. The Franciscan site was granted for the projected residence, but to its rector, who was the theologian Luigi Guala whom we know as an intimate friend and disciple of Lanteri. Since authorization for the Oblates did not come, it was Luigi Guala who began the experiment of a residence on a small scale, by receiving a dozen students for the academic year 1817-1818.

So was born, small but solid, a most useful establishment, and from what we have said there can be no doubt that its father was Bruno Lanteri.

At Carignano

In the summer of 1817 Bruno Lanteri was finally free enough to take direct control of the small community of Oblates in Carignano. Scarcely had he arrived in the midst of his followers when they all went with him into retreat. He knew no other way of beginning a work, and we shall explain in the next chapter how he understood the holy Exercises, how he practiced them and had others follow them, and the fruits he gathered.

He fixed the way of life of his sons definitively. He gave them St. Thomas Aquinas as their first master and St. Alphonsus de Liguori as their second. He wanted them to specialize in popular missions, but in the form of the *Exercises* or a retreat given to a whole parish at one time. They would be assiduous in the confessional. Besides their external apostolate, they would apply themselves solely to prayer and study.

He took care to obtain Pope Pius VII's approval of the king's gift to the congregation of the church of Saint Mary of Graces in Carignano. The Pope received his request most kindly and granted the church all the indulgences that were obtainable there in the time of the Augustinians.

The arrival of Father Lanteri in Carignano was the start of intense activity by the young congregation. The spirit of the whole population was renewed by it. Jansenism had dried out and constricted souls. The sermons and especially the confessional methods of Bruno and his disciples restored liberty to gloomy hearts, opened them to the joy of Christ, made them understand and love the sweetness of Him who said: "My yoke is easy and my burden light!"

A single statistic will suffice to show the progress made: in just one year more than 1,400 people who for decades had not communicated at Easter returned to religious practice.

But Carignano was not enough to satisfy the zeal of the new missionaries. They were in demand in the parishes. They bore throughout Piedmont this spirit of compassion and love, this Christian sense of the sacraments of Penance and especially of the Eucharist, which Jansenist rigorism had ruined almost everywhere. Faith still lived in this hardworking, serious people. The Oblates achieved marvels in the parishes to which they were called. Popular enthusiasm surged up, notably in Monticelli in the diocese of Alba, in Pancalieri in the diocese of Turin, in Fossano and many other places. Young men with vocations began to flock to the newly-founded institute.

It goes without saying that there was also opposition. Satan is always ready to complain about Job's prosperity and to seek permission to test him. As one of Lanteri's biographers says, alongside the triumphant "hosannas" there was more than one "crucify" from the opposing camp. But Father Lanteri knew that even persecution is a source of blessing.

The Storm

If Father Lanteri had had any doubts about this, events were not slow to convince him.

After the congregation's first successes, he judged that the moment had come to work at the definitive erection of the institute on legal bases. He needed two kinds of authorization for this. On the one hand, since he did not want to establish a purely diocesan congregation, limited to the diocese, but a universal one, he needed the approval of the Holy See. On the other hand, the congregation could only obtain civil legality through the government's approval.

Towards the end of 1818 he turned to Rome. The Sacred Congregation of Bishops and Regulars, applying the usual rules in such a case, required the new institute to present first the approval of the new archbishop of Turin. The See had just been filled. The Bishop of Ivrea, Msgr. Colomban Chiaveroti, was named to Turin. He was a zealous man, a former Camaldolese, of strict morals, filled with the need to react against the growing corruption of the time. By reason of the austerity of his life and his inclination to a contemplative life, he tended to consider as a regrettable yielding to the moral decadence of the period the more indulgent methods introduced by an Alphonsus de Liguori in the practice of Penance, even though they had been approved by the Holy See! While finding fault with regalism, the prelate thought all the same that the meddling of the Roman Curia could sometimes be excessive.

For these reasons, which involved the state of his soul and delicate scruples of conscience, the new archbishop was rather reserved about the Oblates from the outset. Instead of answering the Holy See directly, he wrote to Father Lanteri. He praised and approved the zeal of Father Lanteri and his companions. But he declared without equivocation that he absolutely could not approve the new moral doctrines of Alphonsus de Liguori, which he found much too favorable to the general relaxation of morals in the midst of Christianity. He added that he saw no point in a new congregation. The old were amply sufficient. The very most he could allow would be the foundation of a diocesan institute, like the Oblates of St. Charles, established by the great saint who had ruled this church in the sixteenth century.

Father Lanteri was much surprised by such remarks. He replied in two brief letters which were respectfully firm. In the first he pleaded the cause of the new congregation. If there were too many already, none of them was intended for missions to the people, and this new apostolate proved itself indispensable. To do this an institute with a larger base than a single diocese was necessary. In the second letter he defended Liguori's doctrine and pointed out that the Holy See had proclaimed in 1803 that there was nothing deserving censure in it. On the contrary, this doctrine was part of the great Christian tradition of indulgence and kindness to sinners.

The archbishop did not reply to these letters, and two years passed without a decision. The archbishop remained fortified in his opposition. He rejected every request for an audience made by Bruno Lanteri, even when he was traveling through Carignano. He continually expressed his hostility towards the Oblates, when given an opportunity, especially on the subject of their methods of confession. He even tried to turn people influenced by the institute away from it. When they were calumniated, he never came to their defense. Father Lanteri, who was so sensitive, suffered keenly from his archbishop's attitude.

But he could neither disavow his reverence for Alphonsus de Liguori, whom the Church was soon to rank as a saint, nor give up his plan for a universal institute with Pontifical approval. He consoled himself by prayer, and humbly told his sons, "Your strength will be in silence and hope!"

He was encouraged by the archbishop of Genoa, who was later to be Cardinal Lambruschini. The latter, a witness of this poignant drama, was later to say, "Begin the canonization process for Father Lanteri. What I can tell about him will be enough to have him declared Venerable."

But in the long run the situation was becoming almost intolerable. The pastor of Carignano, who was personally a most intransigent rigorist, and who therefore had always been hostile to the congregation in his parish, took advantage of the archbishop's position to foment all sorts of difficulties for and opposition to the Oblates. Insulting posters were put up at night at their door. Obscure threats were made against them.

There was no choice but to give in to the evidence. Life was becoming intolerable. The apostolate of the young congregation was attacked at its roots. Rarely did Bruno Lanteri's humility appear more dazzlingly. Without protest or recrimination, without complaining about the harshness of his adversaries, he did what seemed wisest to him: dissolved his dear congregation!

Dissolution

We can easily guess the dimensions of the tragedy for Father Lanteri in this decision. He himself had to pronounce the death sentence on this congregation which he had not hoped for, which had somehow been thrown into his arms, but whose direction he had assumed so hopefully, this congregation which had had such a fine beginning and which promised so many spiritual benefits. What went on in his soul? Only God knows the secret. Everything was done quietly. The congregation was dissolved in July 1820. Of its members, some went back to their homes, others went to the residence which had just opened in Turin. There they proposed to pursue the holy ministry, around Bruno Lanteri himself, in the church of St. Francis, whose rector was the theologian Guala.

Some Oblates who had been thus dismissed sought to join the Jesuits. There they found the same spirit as animated them in understanding the practice of the sacraments of Penance and the Eucharist.

Would Lanteri Have Become a Jesuit?

Among the documents assembled for the process of beatification of Father Bruno is a series of letters from the Jesuit provincial in Turin, the famous Father Giovanni

Roothan, who was later to become General of the Company. Following two of his dear Oblates, Fathers Antonio Biancotti and Antonio Lanteri, Bruno had begun proceedings to be admitted to the Society. His request was greeted with great respect, even joy. He was too well known, his virtues were of too fine a quality, for his entry into the Company not to be eased in every way, even if it was necessary to ignore some requirements of the Ignatian rule to do so.

But grave objections remained. Without speaking of the important works which Lanteri was still directing in Turin, his discouraging state of health had to be considered. He himself weighed the pros and cons anxiously. Negotiations over his case continued in 1824 and 1825. Finally, to reach a decision, as was essential, he had recourse to his habitual procedure: a good retreat. The *Spiritual Exercises*, which he knew so well, were in principle only a means of choosing the way to accomplish God's will fully. In the middle of May 1825 he went to Chieri, where there was a "probation house" of the Company of Jesus. He performed the Exercises, whose mysteries he had so well penetrated. There he recognized that the will of God was not that he should enter the Jesuit novitiate but that he should do everything possible to restore his dear Company of Oblates.

Once he had reached his decision, he worked wholeheartedly for its fulfillment. Was there still some hope? The congregation, struck down in full flight, had been dissolved for five years. Could it miraculously rise from the tomb? Bruno had confidence only in God. It would be for God to make it possible. But there was a very encouraging indication in the way the Oblates had performed during this dreadful ordeal. We now know that from September 10, 1820 to April 9, 1826, the former members of the congregation, retaining all their veneration for Bruno Lanteri, had ardently continued the kind of apostolate he had inculcated in them, and had given no fewer than 129 retreats for the faithful, 91 of them in the diocese of Turin and the others in 14 neighboring dioceses. Still closely linked to the works created by Father Lanteri, the *Sacerdotal Friendship* and the *Catholic Friendship*, they had meanwhile distributed more than 18,000 copies of good books, as we mentioned earlier.

Thus their courage was great enough. The teams were waiting to reunite. A solution had to be found. And it was on this point that Bruno Lanteri waited for a sign from God.

Resurrection

This sign came at a time when it would have been possible to despair. "The congregation," Father Lanteri gladly said, "is the work of the Madonna. She will be mindful of it!"

Offers·came from various bishops whose judgment on the dissolved society was altogether different from that of the archbishop of Turin. The bishops of Cuneo— which became a see in 1817—of Alba, of Alessandria, and of Novara undertook to give the Society a church and a residence. Each of them had only one desire, to ensure that his diocese benefited from the presence of such a congregation intended for popular missions. Father Lanteri received these invitations, considered the advantages and inconveniences, wisely weighed all the facts bearing on the problem, and waited for God's will to become manifest.

Among those afflicted by his congregation's drama was a very active member of the *Catholic Friendship*, Chevalier Luigi de Collegno. He was a very cultivated man with a deep faith, energetic, prudent and calm. He particularly liked Father Lanteri, whom he considered as a father. He was one of those who tried to help him in the trial he was bearing with such noble patience. God allowed him to think of interesting in the congregation Msgr. Rey, who had just been named—a year before—bishop of Pinerolo, a town in the midst of the valleys of Vaud.

Msgr. Rey had been a very active member of the Chambéry's *Aa*. Bruno Lanteri's name had always been venerated by him. Having devoted himself for many years to the ministry of missions in Savoy, he had no more ardent desire than to establish missionaries in his diocese, where heretics were numerous. The example of Francis de Sales converting the province of Chablais was always before his eyes. Thus, Chevalier de Collegno's proposal fell on a soil that had been prepared. Msgr. Rey, who had long known Bruno Lanteri, hastened to write him a most cordial and affectionate letter to invite him to visit him in Pinerolo to agree on ways to revive the congregation. Father Lanteri quickly sent him the documents necessary to understand the institute, its aims, its spirit, its promising future and the resources it had available. Msgr. Rey carefully studied the papers sent to him. He emerged from this reading not only perfectly clear and satisfied but literally enthusiastic. He extended his protection to the dissolved congregation, and had only one desire, to work for the resurrection of what he already called "the family of my heart."

What proves that at God's sign everything took a triumphal turn is that in September 1825 the bishop of Pinerolo wrote again to Father Lanteri, urging him not to lose a moment in acting, and sending him a letter of approval for the congregation and a petition to forward to the Holy See to obtain pontifical authorization of the Oblates. If we remember that the "retreat of election" made by Father Lanteri over the possibility of entering the Jesuit novitiate, had occurred in May 1825, we can easily measure the intervening progress.

A diocese opened up to the congregation. Possibilities were obvious as far as Rome was concerned. Bruno, always calm and prudent, was letting his decision ripen gradually.

The Jubilee of 1826

In the meantime, Pope Pius VII had died in 1824. His successor was Leo XII, who had celebrated the jubilee of 1825 in Rome and had just extended its preaching to the rest of the Church for 1826. In all directions popular sermons were organized to bring to life again in the people the sense of faith that the Revolution had almost extinguished. Msgr. Rey seized this opportunity to speed approval. He decided to organize a great "mission" at his cathedral in Pinerolo for the benefit of the extraordinary indulgence of the Jubilee and naturally he asked his friend Father Lanteri to provide him with the necessary preachers. Bruno sent him four valiant missionaries: Reynaudi, Loggero, Craveri and Enrico Simonino, the brother of an Oblate who had died shortly before, Filippo Simonino. The bishop welcomed them as ambassadors of God. He wanted to lodge them in his own house and gave them everything they wished for the success of the mission. There was an almost unbelievable attendance. Crowds filled the cathedral and besieged the confessionals. There were very numerous conversions and some of them remarkable because of the scandals which they ended. The bishop was given diplomas and ritual books of freemasonry with which to build a bonfire. A single missionary received more than fifty of them. The Vaudois themselves sometimes came to the sermons. The stirring of faith among Catholics caused a deep emotion. The whole city of Pinerolo displayed the greatest gratitude to the missionaries. Such a success removed all Father Lanteri's hesitations. He understood that God Himself had spoken and wanted the seat of His congregation established in Pinerolo, not Turin.

The Journey to Rome

In this spirit he decided to go to Rome. King Carlo-Felice, learning of these events, supported the request for approval which Father Bruno was going to present to the Holy See, and offered to pay the expense of a journey on a royal frigate from Genoa to Civitavecchia. The most distinguished people in the Kingdom signed petitions to the Holy See at the King's suggestion. When Father Lanteri passed through Genoa, its archbishop, Msgr. Lambruschini, asked him to be his guest.

Accompanied by his faithful Loggero, Father Bruno left for Rome—which in those days was not an easy journey—on April 7, 1826. He arrived on April 20 in the eternal city. He was not unknown there. His zeal for the papacy, the flourishing works he had created in Turin, spoke more eloquently for him and his institute than all the recommendations he brought with him. So his reception in high ecclesiastical spheres was particularly warm. He had been preceded by the request of the bishop of Pinerolo, dated September 10, 1825. It was known that a unanimous vote on October 6 that year by the survivors of the dissolved congregation had elected Father Lanteri as its director, and they had sworn to devote themselves to the congregation and the glory of the Virgin Mary, its protectress.

In response to the first inquiries in Rome, the congregation of Bishops and Regulars, headed by Cardinal Pacca, had already deliberated. It decided in view of the report by its prefect, dated January 20, 1826, to seek more information from the bishop of Pinerolo concerning the rule of the new institute. Father Lanteri's arrival in Rome met the need of the moment. On June 9 the Pope submitted the question of approval to the Congregation of Cardinals. On June 19 he received Father Lanteri and his faithful Don Loggero in a private audience. On July 15 the Congregation advised in favor of the new congregation. On July 21 the Pope ratified its decision and ordered publication of a decree and a brief for its execution.

Everything seemed to be going as well as possible, when an incident occurred which almost stopped everything once more. The secretary of the congregation of Cardinals in charge of the issue, Msgr. Marchetti, was seized by an attack of inopportune zeal. He wanted to impose on the institute a solemn oath to combat the famous Four Propositions containing the doctrine of Gallicanism.

Father Lanteri was willing to take an oath of loyalty to the Holy See, which came to the same thing, but he objected to introducing so specific a change in his rule as was asked of him. He doubted that such an oath was the will of the Holy Father. He held firm. These were miserable days of waiting for him and Father Loggero. But the Virgin was watching over the future institute. The difficulties were finally sorted out. The improper demand that had been made was withdrawn. Finally on September 1, 1826, the brief *Etsi Dei Filius,* approving the congregation, was signed by Cardinal Albano, the secretary of state, and delivered to Father Lanteri the next day.

There were many new difficulties about obtaining the *Exequatur* at the court of Turin. But the King, whom people had tried to turn against the institute, was enlightened by Msgr. Rey during a personal audience on January 22, 1827. The *Exequatur* was promised, and granted shortly afterwards.

Father Lanteri had achieved his objectives. His dear institute was rescued from death, restored to life and set on foot in order to begin its apostolic career.

On July 7, 1827, the Oblates took possession of their house and the church of St. Clare in Pinerolo. Both had been completely refurbished in the meantime at Father Lanteri's expense. On the same day the canonical installation took place joyously. The bishop was overwhelmed with happiness.

But very little time was left for Father Lanteri to build the foundations of his spiritual family.

Before telling the story of his last years—only three remained before his death—and concluding our account, we must try to explain in greater detail the spiritual legacy of the pious founder, the principal inheritance he left his followers when he died.

CHAPTER IX

FATHER LANTERI'S SPIRITUALITY

Schools of Spirituality

Every spirituality amounts in essentials to the union of the soul with God. Only in God can perfect sanctity be found. "Only God is good!" Jesus said. That means, *"Only God is holy,"* in the sense that He alone is holy by His very essence, and that He is the source of all sanctity and all goodness as He is the source of all that is or can be.

Without spending time demonstrating these things we consider irrefutable, we will admit that there are various ways to achieve union with God, to achieve perfection. So there are several "schools of spirituality" in the bosom of genuine spirituality, which is what Christ bequeathed to His Church.

In a substantial work published in France in 1953 with the title *Catholic Spirituality*, eight distinct schools of spirituality are identified, which we shall list in order to introduce the study we shall make in this chapter, the most important in this book, on the Spirituality of Father Lanteri.

According to *Catholic Spirituality*, there are 1) Benedictine spirituality, 2) Franciscan spirituality, 3) Dominican spirituality, 4) Carmelite spirituality, 5) the spirituality of the imitation of Jesus Christ and modern devotion, 6) Ignatian spirituality, 7) St. Francis de Sales' spirituality, and 8) the spirituality of the French school of the seventeenth century.

We should not suppose that this list is exhaustive. It contains only the names of the great schools. Within these schools there is room for considerable variation.

But let us ask to what school Father Lanteri belonged.

A Fervent Ignatian

There can be no doubt about the answer. Of course he venerated all forms of Catholic spirituality. He almost became a Carthusian, which would have tied him more or less to Benedictine spirituality. He was a great admirer of St. Francis of Assisi and his cult of Lady Poverty. In theology he proclaimed himself a disciple of St. Thomas Aquinas. He felt particular devotion for gentle St. Francis de Sales. He often named St. John of the Cross and Saint Teresa of Avila among his preferred saints. He treasured the spiritual riches accumulated by the Church of Christ throughout the ages. But personally, when it was a question of choosing a route to God and to the acquisition of sanctity, he thought he could not do better than to apply himself to the *Exercises* of St. Ignatius. The *Exercises*, to his mind—and we must stress this—said everything and contained everything. It would be impossible to practice the *Exercises* conscientiously without becoming a saint, and he boldly added, "a great saint."

A little book was published in Turin in 1857, which we shall use as thoroughly as possible, called the *Directory for Composing the Exercises of St. Ignatius*. What does this Directory contain? For the most part it is simply an exposition of the contents of the *Exercises* of St. Ignatius, of how to give them and comment on them for the faithful, and to extract all their fruit for oneself.

Fr. Lanteri, in the bottom right-hand corner, advocates the practice of the Spiritual Exercises of Saint Ignatius of Loyola.

When the congregation came into existence, nothing was more urgent than to revive Christian faith. This involved rebuilding a Christian society from the foundations, and carrying out a general reformation of ideas and morals. Father Lanteri had envisioned great things. He could not be accused of limiting his objectives. He went straight for the target. He was convinced that widespread practice of St. Ignatius' *Exercises* was the best means that missionaries could apply to this end.

Listen to him:

"In brief," he wrote, *"St. Ignatius' Exercises are generally a very powerful instrument of divine grace for the universal reformation of the world, and in particular they offer a sure method for everyone to become a saint, a great saint, and to do so speedily."*

In the same context, Father Lanteri declared that that was why he preferred this kind of preaching to all others. For him, we emphasize, this is not just a matter of preaching to the elite, but rather to the masses in the parishes. He conceived a mission to a parish and its ordinary faithful people in the form of the *Exercises,* in a retreat.

This means that he condensed all spirituality, for himself and others, into a more thorough knowledge of the *Exercises.*

We must see therefore how he understood and applied them.

What the *Exercises* Are

Father Lanteri spent his life, it can be said without exaggeration, in going more deeply into the *Exercises.* He saw very well that they are not in any way a sideline of Christian life but are situated at the center of Christian life, that they contain all its vigor, all its meaning, all its substance. To perform the *Exercises,* for Father Lanteri, was to leave the vanities of this world, the shadows and illusions of this earth, to enter the real, the uniquely necessary. The *Exercises* are part of our eternal destiny. They translate the will of God for each of us rigorously and literally, that will of which St. Paul said: *"The will of God is that you should be sanctified!"*

Separated from this will of God, life has no sense or purpose. It is only a passing dream, all too often an absurd nightmare. It is for us to realize its glorious splendor. To do that we must understand and perform the *Exercises*.

Father Lanteri analyzed them minutely. He shows their profound logic. Ignatius starts from the purpose of man. He explains what this purpose is and how it is to be attained. All the *Exercises* are contained in the phrase: to see our end, to realize our goal.

But after this conspectus, Father Lanteri goes into detail.

Division of the *Exercises*

What he saw very well was that the division of the *Exercises* into four weeks is not essentially a temporal but a logical division. It is not necessary to spend four whole weeks performing the *Exercises*. Few of the faithful, few priests even, would be capable of extending them that long. But it is not the four weeks that matter, but the logical development of the thoughts and meditations which make up the *Exercises*.

Once we have understood this point, Father Lanteri judges that there is nothing simpler than to condense the four weeks into eight days—for him the ideal length —or even fewer. Pushing further than him, but in the same direction, we in our turn would say that St. Ignatius' four weeks can easily be condensed into four "movements" of the soul which might usefully fill the single day of recollection which we call "the monthly retreat."

In the practice recommended to his Oblates, however, it is the eight-day retreat which seemed to Father
Lanteri best adapted to everyone's possibilities and needs.

In his wake we shall now rapidly review the work to
be accomplished on each of these eight days.

The Eight-Day Retreat

First day: day of desire—under the protection of
St. Augustine. The purpose of man is considered, as St. Ignatius proposed in the meditation titled *"Foundation"*:
God created us to know Him, love Him, serve Him by always doing His holy will. That is how He wishes to lead
us to our supreme end, which is heaven, or the eternal
possession of God Himself.

Second day: day of compunction—under the protection of St. Peter. We meditate on our failings, those sins
of all sorts into which the devil leads us, which turn us
aside from our purpose. We devote all this second day to
imagining the punishments which sin brings in its train,
the malice included in sin, and consequently the interior
loathing which we must maintain within us concerning sin.

Third day: day of disenchantment—under the protection of St. Francis Borgia. Like the great saint, we
spend this day understanding the vanity of earthly goods,
of fortune, of health, of the pleasures and interests here
below. Most of our sins result from our not thinking
enough about death. It is death which is the great force
for disenchantment. It makes us detached, brings us to
our senses, brings us face to face with the only thing that
is real: *eternal salvation!*

Fourth day: day of fear—under the protection of
St. Jerome. After the serious consideration of death on the
third day, there is nothing as necessary as meditation on
what follows death immediately: judgment; and what

may be the consequence of judgment if we are not careful: hell. But far from leaving souls terrorized, as rigorist preachers did, we must always end this day with the beautiful parable of the prodigal son, placing the meditation devoted to it under the special patronage of St. Mary Magdalene.

We see with what care Father Lanteri poured confidence in divine mercy into sinners' souls.

"Here ends," he said, "the first week, that is, the first part of St. Ignatius' *Exercises*, which corresponds to the purgative way, so called because its objective is to purge or purify the soul of sin and to excite it to sincere contrition by consideration of the four Last Things, and to prepare it for a holy confession."

Fifth day: day of fervor—under the protection of the Holy Family. On this day we meditate on Christ's kingdom. Having hunted sin from our soul, we must give the soul an objective, an ideal, a model for imitation. This model is Jesus Christ. It is of Him that the Father said: *"Ipsum audite!"*

Listen to Him! And He claimed direction of our souls when He said: *"I am the way, the truth and the life!"* and again: *"No man comes to my Father, save by me!"* In Jesus' school we learn to strip off the "old Adam" and to put on the new man.

This day of the retreat is devoted to meditation on the mysteries of the Incarnation and birth of Christ. Here is where we find lessons of humility, detachment and the basic dispositions which make a Christian.

Sixth day: day of devotion—consecrated to meditation on the private or hidden life of Jesus, the thirty years He spent alone in Nazareth, and then on His public life, so as to harvest for our souls all the examples Christ left us. "Put on the Lord Jesus Christ," St. Paul said. And again "Let Jesus' life be shown forth in your bodies!"

Seventh day: day of energy—under the protection of Our Lady of the Seven Sorrows. Meditation on the passion of Jesus Christ. We find the energy to struggle against temptation and to bear the trials of life in the spectacle of our Divine Master at grips with suffering and death.

Eighth day: day of joy—under the protection of all heaven's angels and saints.

The second and third weeks of St. Ignatius' *Exercises*, which correspond to the *illuminative way*, so called because it is in this part of our interior life that Jesus Christ, the true light, "illumines every man who comes into the world," conclude on this day.

But Jesus is not only light, He is also warmth. If He illumines, He also warms and sets aflame. He said Himself: *"I came to cast fire on the earth."*

The meditations intended to carry us to love are first about paradise. St. Paul wants our thought to be always on Jesus resurrected: "If you are resurrected with Christ," he said, "seek the things above, love the things above, and not those on earth below."

A second meditation on the same day is devoted to *love of God*. Everything must be done out of love. Nothing is difficult for him who loves. Everything must therefore converge on love. St. Augustine's famous remark: *Love and do as you will* is a good summary of Christian life.

Here ends the fourth and last week of St. Ignatius' *Exercises*.

Supplementary Meditations

Those who know St. Ignatius' *Exercises* may well be astonished not to find in the plans which fill these eight days some famous themes, such as the "Two Standards" and the "Three Types of Men." But we must remember what is very important—that Father Lanteri, in this exposition, is showing his missionaries the program they must follow in preaching to the masses. It is clear that they must limit themselves to the most elementary and basic truths. But whenever the *Exercises* are given to more educated audiences or to those called to higher perfection, especially to priests or to groups of laymen genuinely seeking God, at least one day must be given to the following three meditations which are so prominent in St. Ignatius' text: the *Two Standards*, the *Three Types of Men*, the *Three Degrees of Humility*.

But here we must make a very important observation.

A reader who has read through the eight days of the *Exercises* above may have thought that they scarcely surpassed the most commonplace spirituality. Had Father Lanteri gone no further than this? Did he limit himself to these teachings, no doubt very sound but really common among the most ordinary Christians, even catechism children? Certainly not! What he said or recommended should be said during the *Exercises* was the core of his faith and his interior life. He was not practicing *esoterism*. But he did not lose sight of the fact that Jesus Himself distinguished between obeying the commandments, which is *required*, and the quest for perfection, which is *recommended*: "If you wish to be perfect!" He said to the young man who questioned Him about the way of achieving eternal life.

But this distinction between precept and counsel, between the quest for eternal life and that for perfection, does not oblige us, in Father Lanteri's thought, to desert Ignatius' *Exercises*. He found everything in this little book. It was written not only for simple Christians, but also for souls consecrated to the Lord. We need only go further into the spirit of its holy author.

The meditations on the Two Standards, on the Three Types of Men, on the Three Degrees of Humility, will serve perfectly those who wish to rise higher than requirements and attain to the practice of what is recommended.

The *Two Standards*, we know, are those of Satan and Jesus Christ. We must enlist with one or the other. St. Augustine argued that we must choose between two Cities, the City of good or the City of evil, the City of God or of the devil. In Father Lanteri's commentaries on the Two Standards, there are magnificent flights toward perfection. If he truly spoke from the soul in his preachings to the people, he did so much more deeply in his retreats preached to elites.

The meditation on the *Three Types of Men*, equally Ignatian, served in his mind to distinguish the degrees by which one rises to divine union: the first type of men, he said with St. Ignatius, are sick and wish to be healed but refuse to take the necessary medicines. Their will to be whole is only a vain longing and is of no service to God. The second type resembles sick people who wish to be healed and who swallow the necessary medicines, but prefer those that taste sweet and neglect the others. They wish to be whole, but their limited, conditional desire is easily diverted by the difficulties in the way. Such a will is still inadequate to reach our goal.

Finally the third type of men is that of the sick who are determined to be made whole and are prepared to accept any medicine, even if it is unpleasant. This kind of will is the only one which permits proper service to God and true imitation of Jesus Christ.

Even this will has varying degrees. The objective of the meditation on the *Three Degrees of Humility* is to reveal these different stages on the way to high perfection.

The first degree of humility consists in being ready to sever oneself from everything created, renouncing the goods of the world, bearing everything and confronting death itself rather than offend God by mortal sin.

The second degree consists in behaving the same way to avoid even voluntary venial sin.

The third and last degree, which leads directly to sainthood, consists, in addition to fleeing even venial sin, in feeling oneself inwardly disposed to embrace, when God shows it to be His will, poverty, humiliation, suffering, and death itself in order to imitate Jesus Christ more perfectly.

This third degree is the objective to which St. Ignatius definitely intends to bring the person on retreat doing the *Exercises*. But not everyone is fit. That is why meditations of this nature are reserved for those who sincerely wish to become saints.

Here Father Lanteri shows us the uttermost depths of his soul. He had experienced the heroic virtues above and beyond ordinary virtues. No doubt that was not his purpose, but his passionate love of the *Exercises* reveals to us what in him was most intimate and fruitful.

That leads us to raise the most delicate of questions: *did Father Lanteri know the peaks of mystical life?*

Lanteri a True Mystic?

Such a question may seem strange to some of our readers. The word *mystic* is so often misused, is used in so many different senses, and, if one may say so, is served up so variously, that many people do not know what we mean by this question.

The *mystical* life begins where the simply *ascetic* life ends. It is characterized by the predominance of *passive prayer* over the ordinary *Ignatian meditation*. St. John of the Cross complained many times, in his sublime theological works, about those directors of conscience who, paying little attention to the signs which show God's summons to high sanctity, limit their pupils by force to the practice of *discursive meditation*, without allowing them to leave the way free for divine grace, which would raise them to higher levels of prayer, the *prayer of quiet*, above all *the prayer of union.*

No one has explained the differences between these kinds of supernatural prayer and ordinary meditation better than St. Teresa in her famous *Libro de su Vida.*

Basically she said that we should compare the practice of prayer with the watering of a garden. There are four ways of watering. First, we can water with water drawn with effort from the bottom of a well. This is ordinary meditation, which is achieved arduously with the collaboration of all our faculties: memory, intelligence, will. But we can also water with a "noria," a device which provides water easily and more abundantly. This method is better and more effective than the first. It supposes that divine grace comes to the aid of our faculties with much more force and effectiveness. Third, we can water by irrigation, by a stream or canal bringing water without the gardener exerting himself. This is the image of the *prayer of quiet*, in which God keeps the soul at peace without it needing to apply its faculties and even withdrawing from it the power to do so, holding it simply but firmly subjected to His supernatural action. Finally, there is a fourth way of watering a garden, the coming of a heavy rain sent by the Lord. This fourth method, which symbolizes the highest forms of contemplative prayer, is by far the happiest and most fruitful of all.

Having summarized the sublime insights of Saint Teresa on these degrees of prayer, let us return to Father Lanteri. We have asked: *was Father Lanteri a mystic?* By that we meant, did he know the highest forms of prayer, or did he remain limited to laborious, slow meditation of

the kind described in St. Ignatius' *Exercises?* This raises
the question of St. Ignatius' contemplative life itself. It
raises the question whether there is room in the Ignatian
Exercises for the soaring flights of mystic life. Those who
know the history of mystical theology are not unaware
that this question has been passionately debated, in the
past, even in the bosom of the Company of Jesus.

But two things seem generally agreed on nowadays:
1) that Ignatius—and Father Lanteri too—only performed the Exercises to cover the essential stages of Christian and religious life. That is why he proposes to people
on retreat only ordinary meditation, which consists in
watering the garden with water drawn with effort from
the well of the soul.

2) But he knew very well—as did Father Lanteri—
from personal experience the higher stages of the soul's
ascension towards God. He left open the doors of contemplative life. Better still, he opened the doors himself, at
the end of the *Exercises*, through the "contemplation of
love." In other words, he did not restrict himself to the
purgative way, that of the first week of the Exercises,
nor to the *illuminative way*, that of the second and third
weeks of the *Exercises*, but he led his retreatant to the
summits of the *unitive way*, and that was the purpose of
his fourth week.

Conclusive Signs

As concerns our hero, the best indications lead us to
believe that he raised himself and his pupils, according to
their aptitudes, to the highest peaks of unitive life.

Here are the indications, at least the main ones.

In the first place, all the texts we have agree that he
had his own special way of giving the *Exercises*. In his
mouth, the retreat meditations had a special savor. What
did his originality consist in? Witnesses of his life tell us

that *"he began the* Exercises *where others ended them."*
This is unusually eloquent. Others stopped with the concluding meditation on divine love. But with Lanteri one
was plunged in this love from the beginning. In other
words, one felt plunged with him, from the start, in the
sweetness of divine love, that means, we cannot doubt, in
the unitive life.

And that is a very precious indication. But there is
another, which to us seems even more persuasive.

Wishing to glean the practice of the *Exercises*, which
for him were the *Summa* of mystical theology, he arrived
at the following table of four movements of the soul cor-
responding to the four weeks of the retreat:

1. *Deformatum reformare,*
2. *Reformatum conformare,*
3. *Conformatum confirmare,*
4. *Confirmatum transformare.*

In English: 1) reform the deformed, 2) conform the
reformed, 3) confirm the conformed, 4) transform the
confirmed!

The reform of what was deformed is the purgative
way, the first movement or week of the Exercises.
To conform to Christ, the supreme model, what has been
reformed, is the illuminative way, and the second movement. To confirm in itself what has been conformed to
the divine model, is the summit of the illuminative way.
But the unitive way, high perfection, great sanctity, is the
fourth movement: *transforming what has been confirmed.* In this single word, transform, we can include all
the degrees of sanctity, however high. Father Lanteri
thus led his penitent to the highest peaks of the contemplative life. That implies that he himself had experienced
these admirable peaks!

Finally, the third indication, which seems to us decisive, is his way of speaking of divine love.

There are emphases which do not deceive. Our Lord said: "The mouth speaks from the heart's abundance." The highest mystical life is necessarily translated by the highest flights of love. The thermometer of sanctity is the degree of love burning in the heart.

That is why, when we hear Bruno Lanteri speaking of love in terms we shall quote, we conclude: behold, that which we were seeking:

"Without the inward spirit," he often said, *"we will never do anything, there must be fire, fire, fire, an intense and heroic love of God, but the spirit of God is order and calm!...*

We have asked: was Lanteri a mystic? Here is our answer. Only a mystic, and a great mystic, can speak in this way: *"Fire, fire, fire!"*

This cry from the uttermost depths of the soul is an exclamation which cannot deceive. Mystics are all brothers in love. Father Bruno Lanteri was an emulator of the great mystics of the Christian ages, because he had this sense of love, because he had this cult of "fire," that fire of which Christ said: *"I came to cast fire on earth, and what do I desire but that it be kindled?"*

After this brief study of his spirituality, we must consider his last years on earth and see him grappling with that which carries us from the shadows of this life to the splendors of eternal glory: *death.*

CHAPTER X

LAST YEARS AND DEATH OF FATHER LANTERI (1827-1830)

On the Threshold of Death

Father Lanteri spent his three last years in Pinerolo, now the seat of his dear congregation. He had worn out his remaining strength in confirming his work. His health had never been good, as we know. After his journey to Rome in 1826 and the authorization of his dear Oblates in 1827, he could sing his *nunc dimittis*. It seemed to him that his work on earth was finished.

His visitors unanimously recorded his exhaustion. In April, 1829, Marquis Michele de Cavour, who had come to see him, wrote: "The Superior, Father Lanteri, is very gentle, but his health could not be worse...he could scarcely draw breath. 'The lamp is going out,' he told me. His face showed him at peace."

As the months passed he became weaker. At the beginning of 1830 his health was in a dreadful state: the pressure on his chest, unquestionably asthma, was more and more distressing. His sight was almost gone. His stomach rejected almost any nourishment. He was subjected to a ceaseless martyrdom by all sorts of hidden infirmities. It was left to him to show the strength of the spirit of faith and love living in him through his patience and courage in suffering. To the very end, as far as he was able, he remained faithful to the rules of their community. When he was forced to stay in his bed, no longer able to read to himself, he had himself read to by the brother coadjutor who helped him in his illness, Pietro Gardetti, or by Father Michele Valmino. They helped him with the required meditation, spiritual reading, visits to the Holy Sacrament, and recitation of the rosary.

His life had become a continuous prayer. Thanks to a touching idea, he had a little window made in the wall of his bedroom through which he could see the tabernacle where his Jesus reposed in the adjacent chapel. He talked to Him through prayer, tears and uninterrupted conversations. Having lived in love, he was preparing himself in this way for what St. John of the Cross calls "death in love," and which he proclaimed the only death appropriate for a true friend of our Lord.

What he repeated most often, in the form of ejaculatory prayer, was the Latin saying: "*O bone Jesu, sitio Te!*" "O dear Jesus, I thirst for You."

One of his greatest joys was to feel himself so near the Holy Sacrament. "*Oh! Pietro,*" he would say to his nurse, Brother Gardetti, "*what grace the Lord showed me in placing Jesus in the tabernacle so close to me!*"

When he could no longer speak and his sight was almost gone, he put on his spectacles to look in the direction of the tabernacle and to enter a silent dialogue of looks and outbursts of love with his Jesus.

We asked in the preceding chapter if he had been elevated to the mystic state. All the characteristics we describe now confirm most strikingly the affirmative answer we have given to this question. Such beautiful love of the Eucharistic Jesus is the sign of the mystic state. But above all this continuity in love, in the feeling of the divine presence, is the certain sign of a life in mystic union with God. Let us remember the definition of mystic life given by St. John of the Cross: *"Habitual attentiveness, loving and peaceful, to the presence of God in the heart."* That is exactly what we find in Father Lanteri on his deathbed: he thinks only of God, his God is always with him, and he adores Him continually, but all in the most perfect peace! Let us note that he could not have been granted such grace at this supreme hour unless he had prepared himself by a very similar life. To die in love one must have lived in love. Such was indeed Bruno Lanteri's life, for such was his death.

Final Visits

Among the last joys given him in these final months of his life, we must list some memorable visits. At the beginning of June, Canon Luigi Craveri came. He was one of Lanteri's favorite disciples. Craveri has left us the most moving testimony about his dear master, and this testimony is part of the process of beatification. He does not hesitate to call Lanteri "a great man, who even performed miracles, and who died in the odor of sanctity." For a long while Craveri had wished to enter the congregation. He was only prevented by the opposition of his archbishop in Turin, who, after two years of silence, had finished by answering his letters: "Frightened by your reasons, I consent, but I do not approve!"

Bruno Lanteri had the highest esteem for him. He believed that his vocation came genuinely from God, and in his opinion Craveri should have taken over direction of the congregation after his death.

"In this last interview," Craveri writes, "he told me that if I had chosen to join the congregation at once, this would have been the case, but that now it was too late. And he showed me, by a gesture, that he was going to be buried. Indeed, he died two months after."

Msgr. Rey, who at this time was transferred to the see of Annecy, and several other bishops also came to see him. His friends, the theologians Guala, Daverio, Zorgniotti and others too, came to tell him how much they wished he could complete his work. They jested by assuring him that he would live another twenty years, and that only then would they discuss whether he could be spared!

But he, thanking them with a smile, answered simply: "I feel my strength weakening day by day and I am ready to sacrifice my life."

To his sons he declared: *"I am not the founder of this congregation, but the Blessed Virgin Mary is its Foundress and Mother: she will continue to govern it as she always has."*

Devotion to Mary held a like place in his heart to devotion to the Eucharist. He called her his Lady, his Mother, his Paradise. And from words which escaped him his followers concluded that he had several times had the consolation of her visible presence beside him: "I see," he happened to say, "a beautiful Lady with a beautiful Child in her arms, and she never leaves me!"

Last Mass, Last Communion

As long as he had the strength, he had celebrated holy Mass each day without fail. The last day on which he could do this was the Feast of St. Joseph, March 19, 1830. He had always said, "I hope I shall still be able to celebrate Mass on March 19." He began the Mass and said it as far as the Gospel. Then he had a collapse and had to rest a while. But strength returned to him and he could go on to the end. Overjoyed, he told Brother Pietro: "St. Joseph obtained for me the grace I desired so much!"

Afterwards he wanted to try to celebrate Mass again, but at the epistle he felt ill. He had to be relieved of his vestments and carried to his room. From then on he had to give up going to the holy altar. He received Communion every day, attending from his bed the Mass celebrated by his dear Father Valmino in the nearby chapel. Because of his strictness of conscience he was accustomed to confess every day.

The prayer he loved so much: "O dear Jesus, I thirst for You!" came to his mind more and more and hastened to his lips. Every day his strength lessened, but there was no sign that his death was imminent.

Even his last night was calm and peaceful. But he had not waited until he felt in extremity to ask for Extreme Unction. He had received it some days before in intense piety. Besides, his every moment was from then on consecrated to prayer. To encourage this he willingly revered pious images, those of the Virgin or saints, and above all his crucifix. Throughout his life, one of the most reliable witnesses of his daily habits, Father Ferrero, tells us, he had placed himself purely on the supernatural plane, "seeking always to act exclusively for God. His only fear," the same witness specifies, "even in his last illness, was that he might not act for a supernatural purpose and for the greater glory of God." And Father Ferrero adds: "When he was on the threshold of death, we saw him smile when someone encouraged him to have confidence."

As was his practice, he had confessed again the day before his death. On the morning of August 5, 1830, he could once more attend, as he did every day, Mass celebrated by Father Valmino, and he received Holy Communion. Everything went on so normally that no one thought his last hour was near. While he was offering his thanks and talking intimately and silently to the Eucharistic Jesus, the brother with him asked if he needed anything.

"Nothing," he answered peacefully.

But a few moments later, he signalled to the brother to come near. The latter repeated his question and asked what he wanted. He answered that he wanted nothing:

"But," he added with a gasp, *"I see a Lady who puts a Child on my chest and at the same time I can breathe no more!"*

"Perhaps it is the Madonna paying you a visit," answered good Brother Pietro with a smile.

Father Bruno smiled in his turn. His face was marked with sweetness, his glance was towards heaven, and his whole attitude spoke of a motionless ecstasy.

Only then did the brother guess that perhaps his end was approaching. He hastened to summon the community. All hurried in, deeply moved. It was about eight in the morning when the Father went into agony. All his sons were there, round his bed, crying and praying, and begging a last blessing from him. One of the Fathers supported the dying man's arm so that he could bless them all. He was fully conscious and his paternal gesture was accompanied by most affectionate expressions. His last words were what one would expect from a heart full of love, from a servant of God, at the moment of accomplishing his "death in love":

"Love one another, love one another profoundly, and always remain one at heart, whatever it may cost you!"

Gathered around him, they began to recite the prayers for the dying. When they came to these words from the Gospel according to St. John:

"Holy Father, keep in your name those you have given me, that they may be one as we are one,"

the dying man made a sign to repeat this prayer of the Divine Master. Scarcely had this phrase been repeated when the venerated Father was seen to look a last time, radiant with love, towards the tabernacle; then, with a sweet smile, without any sign of suffering, he breathed his last.

Death at once dressed his face with incomparable beauty. White and rose, it was the face of a man plunged in the most tranquil sleep. Only then was it possible to have an experienced painter do his portrait. An incredible sweetness predominates in the pictures we have of him. His eyes are direct and pure; the lips express an affectionate smile. His features are a little thin but regular and compassionate and express goodness more than anything, but less an ordinary, purely human goodness than a supernatural charity, a profound love nourished by Christ's infinite charity.

This happy death came at about nine o'clock on the morning of August 5, 1830. Bruno Lanteri, born on May 12, 1759, had completed his seventy-first year by a little less than three months.

The unanimous feeling of those present at his death was that they had just lost a "saint." All wished to have something to remember him by, such as a relic. His funeral was a triumph. His body was laid to rest in the church of St. Clare, and he lay there until 1901, when, in view of the beatification process, it was identified before being transported to the sanctuary erected by his dear Oblates for the glory of the Sacred Heart. A second identification of the body took place for the informative process on September 18, 1926.

EPILOGUE

The friends of Father Lanteri await with perfect confidence the Church's verdict on the heroic nature of his virtues and on the miracles obtained by his intercession. We hope we can number the readers of this book among his friends. It is impossible to survey this life which is so beautiful, so upright, so perfect, without being filled with sympathy and veneration for the true priest of Christ that Father Lanteri was.

Holy Scripture, speaking of the just, likes to use comparisons drawn from the growth of a fine tree: the palm tree which flowers, the Lebanon cedar or the plane-tree which grows beside a river. If we understand these images aright, they mean that the just man dies where he has taken root. Father Lanteri did not waver from his first aspirations. He had taken root, on the day of his birth, in Jesus Christ, thanks to baptismal regeneration. Rooted in Christ, he developed into a fine tree, its trunk rising towards the sky, its branches stretching out in broad harmonious foliage, its blossoms and fruits pleasing to all eyes.

Theologians and canon lawyers who will examine his virtues will have no trouble, turning the pages of his life, in discovering on each of them evident proofs of his faith, his hope, and his charity, both sweet and ardent. All the other virtues—humility, poverty, religion, prudence, justice, perfect purity of morals—are equally to be found, supported by abundant and certain witnesses. His courage will be glorified, especially for the predominant part he played in the struggle against antireligious persecution, against the errors of his time, against all the enemies of the faith and the Church.

But if there were one consideration that should tip the balance with a view to his beatification, it is what we would call his relevance to the times. More than ever we need holy priests and laymen who are generous and devoted to the Church and the Holy See. No one was more careful than he was about priestly sanctity, no one worked more happily than he did to organize Catholics for apostolic action on all the social levels of his day. No one saw more justly or more sensibly, nor practiced more resolutely, the methods appropriate to our time for the defense and triumph of Christian truth. He was the principal initiator of what we call the apostolate of the press. Throughout his life he worked to propagate good literature, the only effective remedy against the torrent of foul literature which corrupts and poisons spirits.

Justly we may call Lanteri the father of Catholic Action in Italy. Concerning this we cannot do better than to quote the opinion of a great Pope, recorded by one of the newest biographers of Father Lanteri, Father Paolo Calliari of the Congregation of Oblates of the Virgin Mary.

It happened in 1927. The leaders of Catholic Action in Italy had just held their annual assembly in the presence of Pope Pius XI. After reading the reports, the Holy Father, descending from his throne, went and mingled familiarly with the people of the congress. Suddenly, the voice of a university student was heard as he shouted in a moment of silence from the other end of the hall:

"Most Holy Father, give us a protector!"

He meant: give Catholic Action in Italy a cardinal-protector. At the same time, the student looked in the direction of Cardinal Serafini, who was present.

The Pope seemed to think for a moment about the appeal directed to him, then, raising his voice, he said forcefully:

"As long as we live, the protector *of Catholic Action will be the Pope!*"

Then, after a silence, raising his head and his hand, he added:

"Pray the Lord that Father Pio Bruno Lanteri may soon be raised to the altar: he would be the natural protector of Catholic Action, as it now exists."

Let us obey that great Pope, Pius XI, and pray the Lord that Father Lanteri may soon be for us *Blessed Bruno Lanteri!*

On the Feast of the Immaculate Conception, December 8, 1955

MISSIONARY DIMENSION OF FATHER LANTERI IN THE BEGINNINGS OF THE CATHOLIC CHURCH OF NORTH AMERICA

by Father Paolo Calliari, O.M.V.

The Missionary Spirit of the *Anonymous Friendship*

It might seem that Father Lanteri's total involvement in the cultural and religious problems which troubled Piedmont, Italy and France would have caused him to forget the problems of the universal Church. One might say, Father Lanteri did not dedicate enough effort to the "Catholic" dimension of evangelization and pastoral action which the missionary apostolate required at that time. However, this is not the case. The entire spiritual formation of Lanteri was distinctively missionary in the broadest and most modern sense of the word. From the time of his university studies and especially during his years of formation in the school of Father Diessbach, Lanteri shows an ever increasing missionary zeal.

The "brothers" of the *Anonymous Friendship* in Turin were closely involved with foreign missions. This group, which was under Lanteri's direction and incentive for thirty years, corresponded with the missionaries of Asia and of North and South America. They received information from these missions and communicated their news to others showing the deep and sincere missionary spirit of the *Friendship.*

One of the books which re-enkindled the people's interest in the missions at the end of the 17th century was entitled: *Lettres edifiantes et curieuses, ecrites des Missions etrangeres par quelques Missionares de la Compagnie de Jesus* (Edifying and interesting notes concerning foreign missions, written by some missionaries of the Company of Jesus). These notes filled a total of 28 volumes and, in spite of their bulk, reached a wide diffusion. They were also translated into other languages and effectively contributed to making the Catholic missions known and loved.

Father Lanteri, the brothers of the *Friendship,* and later on the *Christian Friends* made it their duty to spread these volumes of missionary letters among the people with every means available to them.

The Fall of Missionary Activity in the 17th Century

The missionary spirit, though deep and very much alive during the life of Father Lanteri, was capable of effecting very little in the troubled times in which he lived.

The last ten years of the 17th century and the early years of the 18th century reveal what was the highpoint in missionary decay in Europe and in other Catholic nations. This was evidenced by the general indifference in public opinion for missionary problems and the grave lack of priests in mission countries (they had dwindled at this time to a few hundred who were abandoned to themselves). This was largely due to the events which were taking place at that time which affected even the Popes, Pius VI and VII. The decay of the missionary effort was the fruit of the anti-religious propaganda and the anti-Catholic movement of "Illuminism." In addition, the Encyclopedia and school of Voltaire presented the Catholic missionary as the breeder of superstition, an agent of colonialism and the corrupter of the idyllic customs of the "good savages." Other factors in missionary decay were the French Revolution which had held captive the minds and hearts of all Europeans for a decade and the Napoleonic regime which in many ways had brought the Church to faithfully copy its programs and methods of revolution.

This threefold crisis, then, had inflicted a blow to the missions which seemed to be fatal: turmoil existed in the religious, social and political realms. In such conditions any real involvement in missionary activity outside of one's own country was practically impossible.

It was not until the pontificate of Gregory XII (1831-1846) that a reawakening to missionary problems took place. From this time on, throughout all of the 18th and 19th centuries and down to our own days nothing would hinder the missionary effort.

Daniel-Rops states that: "The history of the Catholic missions in the 19th century is an extraordinary and wonderful one. It is one of the most impressive witnesses which can be set forth to illustrate the Church's vitality, its perennial youthfulness and capacity for heroism and tenacity."[1]

In the early years of the 18th century the missionary comeback was still incipient and almost dormant, but some visible signs already in motion gave promise of a future resurrection. It would not be an exaggeration to say that within the territory of Piedmont one of the most involved workers for this missionary resurrection was Father Lanteri. The work was carried out both by Father

Lanteri and by the group of *Friends* of which he was the head. In a certain sense it can be said that Lanteri was the bridge that united the missionary activity of the 17th century with that of the early 18th century. We will see this more clearly in the section of this chapter which treats of an area of his life which is still little known: the "missionary" dimension of his priestly apostolate.

The Missionary and Ecclesial Dimensions

The missionary dimension stems from the ecclesial dimension. This means that the importance and the urgency of the missions is born and develops through an ecclesiology which is properly understood. If the Church must be, as it truly is, the "Sacrament of Salvation" for all men, then the Lord's precept to "Go and preach the Good News" remains valid for all times. The vast and profound ecclesiology of Father Lanteri could not but bring him to an ever more "catholic" view of the Church, that is, a universal view. He envisioned this universality in the duties which Christ entrusted to His Church. Furthermore, he recognized the need of an ever deeper and more effective penetration of the salvific message throughout the world and in all of humanity.

Such was the missionary concern that moved Lanteri and weighed upon him, that at one time he himself desired to join the courageous pioneers of the missions in order to bring the salvific message to distant lands. He wrote in 1816:

"If my age and illnesses did not prevent me, I would readily offer my services to the missions, and I would consider myself fortunate to be able to supply the needs of this expedition, but since I am unable to do this, I must be satisfied to offer myself, always ready to receive your commands."[2]

These words were directed toward the French bishop who is considered one of the principal founders of the Catholic Church in the United States, Bishop Louis Guillaume-Valentine du Bourg (1766-1833), the first bishop of New Orleans in Louisiana. The mission area that Father Lanteri would have liked to go to, if his health and age permitted it, was precisely the vast region which at that time was called Louisiana. It extended from Canada to the Gulf of Mexico and from the Mississippi Valley to the Rocky Mountains, comprising a tenth of the area which is now the United States.

It is difficult today, after more than a century, to follow one by one the traces which the remote apostle, Lanteri, left on the land of Missouri, Wisconsin, Michigan, Quebec and Louisiana proper, but this does not mean that his apostolate did not effectively exist or that it did not bring abundant fruit.

The Louisiana Mission Territory

Following the fall of the French power in 1763, in the New France, as Canada was called, and in the French territories of North America, the situation of Catholics became ever more alarming by the lack of religious assistance after the massive exodus of French priests and insufficient recruiting of new vocations. The Quebec Act of 1773 signed by George III of England rendered the situation less precarious inasmuch as it facilitated the immigration of other Catholic missionaries from Europe, but it did not entirely normalize the situation. During the revolution and under the regime of Napoleon, some French priests were able to reach America but not in the needed measure. Among these were the Sulpician Fathers and Jesuits.

After Napoleon fell, the relation between Europe and America was felt more keenly and so also was the need for its evangelization. One of the most outstanding of those soliciting missionaries for America was certainly Du Bourg.

Du Bourg in Italy and in Turin

Ordained a priest in France in 1788, Du Bourg fled to Spain when the revolution erupted and from there went to America—to Baltimore in Maryland—and was welcomed there by the Fathers of St. Sulpicius, the congregation into which he would go in 1795.

In Baltimore he was at first a teacher in the celebrated Georgetown College, founded by Bishop John Carroll. Later he himself founded a college which became St. Mary's Seminary. He knew St. Elizabeth Anne Seton, foundress of the Daughters of Charity. He directed her spiritually and is considered in a certain sense the co-founder of Mother Seton's Daughters. His uncommon gifts of intelligence and heart impressed Bishop Carroll who in 1812 nominated him administrator of the territory of Louisiana sold by Napoleon to the United States nine years earlier, in 1803.

For three years Du Bourg carried the weight of a very large diocese, four times the size of France and deprived of priests—he had only about a dozen priests who were all elderly—where the practice of the Christian life was non-existent and the divisions among the faithful as well as the attempts at schism were frequent.

During the autumn of 1815, Du Bourg came to Rome and explained to Pius VII his situation. He asked either to be released from a burden too great to carry or to be given priests proportionate to the need. Pius VII encouraged him to stay at his post, had him consecrated bishop of Louisiana (the first bishop of the area) and authorized him to seek missionaries and money to meet his most urgent needs. Divine Providence aided him in both undertakings, allowing him to find a good group of missionaries among the Italian religious (the Lazarines most of all) and also among the diocesan clergy. Divine Providence allowed him to find generous persons and offerings of money for his work. Among the first missionaries was also the Piedmontese Father Felice de Andreis (1778-1820) of Demonte near Cuneo, the beatification of whom is in progress.

Du Bourg and Lanteri

In his search for missionaries, Du Bourg arrived on March 1, 1816, in Turin to meet with the *Christian Friendships* and, in particular, with the Marchise Cesare d'Azeglio, to whom he had been recommended. Under such circumstances it was inevitable that he would have met with Father Lanteri also. The influence and prestige which Lanteri enjoyed in this subalpine capital would be a valid help towards the ends which the missionary bishop wished to reach.

Right away Lanteri made his own the problems, intentions and preoccupation of Du Bourg and, as the practical man he always was, gave his collaboration on four matters which seemed to him most urgent and which were later shown to be most useful for the young mission: he recruited missionary personnel, gathered funds, sent religious books and urged a struggle against the newly formed biblical societies. Nor was this quadruple form of collaboration limited to the time Du Bourg was in Europe (he left for New Orleans June 17, 1817), but it continued for about ten years uninterruptedly by means of the *Catholic Friendship* (which succeeded the *Christian Friendship* in 1817) and the work of the Propagation of the Faith which he, with d'Azeglio and others, was able to introduce to Piedmont in 1824.

Du Bourg and Lanteri Collaborate

The missionaries that Lanteri initially found for Bishop Du Bourg were four, all coming out of the association for priests directed by him and which we already mentioned: the Pious Union of St. Paul. Different difficulties, arising at the last moment, seemed to prevent some from leaving, but then the difficulties were resolved easily. The missionaries from Lanteri all made out very well in the new land.[3] His own secretary, Don Giuseppe Loggero, later attempted to join, but it did not come about. As we have seen, Lanteri himself would have liked to put himself at the head of this new squadron of evangelical workers, but, in his condition of health, it would have been foolish for him to think of attempting such an undertaking.

At first Lanteri occupied himself personally with the gathering of funds for the new mission and with positive results. But later on, this particular form of missionary help was carried on by the *Catholic Friends* under the direction of Cesare d'Azeglio, a praiseworthy layman in many areas but particularly for his valid contribution to the propagation of the ideal of the missionary spirit in Piedmont.

The Book Apostolate in America

To the *Catholic Friends* is owed also the great help given to the diocese of New Orleans, and other neighboring dioceses, in the form of catechetical, devotional and apologetical books. In the minutes of the *Catholic Friendship* there are mentioned thousands of copies of books in French sent from Turin to Monsignor Luigi Leopold Moni (1782-1842), Vicar General of Bishop Du Bourg, by means of the Sardinian general consul in Philadelphia, Gaspare Deabbate.

Furthermore, the Bishop of Baltimore, Ambrose Marechal (1764-1828), and then his successor Bishop James Withfield (1770-1834), and even the Bishop of Cincinnati Edward Fenwick, O.P. (1768-1832), turned to the *Catholic Friendship* of Turin for subsidies of books for the use of the clergy and for the superior schools of their dioceses, and their desires were in part satisfied. In this book initiative, Lanteri appeared little; in fact his name is never officially mentioned, but it is evident that his council and his encouragement had a decisive effect in an apostolate that was always dear to him. Where, on the other hand, his personal intervention appears manifest is in the struggle against the Biblical Society founded in London in 1804 which, strengthened by abundant financial means, sought to penetrate the Catholic populations of Louisiana.

Lanteri had reprinted the *Letter of Fenelon to the Bishop of Arras on the Reading of the Bible* and the *Brief Exposition of the Marks of the True Religion* of Cardinal Gerdil, and he sent several thousand copies of them to New Orleans.

He himself wrote a booklet to make known the origin, methods of propaganda, dangers and evils caused by some organizations.

There was also projected, in accordance with the *Catholic Friends*, a French edition of the New Testament for the exclusive benefit of the Catholics of Louisiana, but for diverse reasons the initiative had to be put off and it seems that in the end it was not able to be effected.

The missionary dimension or the "catholic" viewpoint of the Church was certainly not lacking in Lanteri. It is characteristic that it was shown in the vast region of North America, destined to reach, in the turn of a century, a tremendous development. He, from afar, knew how to sow in those regions seeds which would germinate and bring forth abundant fruit. American Catholicism ought to give recognition to the silent and obscure action of this humble priest of Turin: we will not be able to say in what measure that seed may have borne fruit—God alone knows—it is certain, however, that it was not put into the ground in vain.

Thus, even the missionary dimension of Lanteri, expressed in an active and practical form, serves to shed new light on his personality already so rich and complex and on his spirituality so typically ecclesial and "catholic."

FOOTNOTES

1. Daniel-Rops, *L'Eglise des Revolutions* (Paris, 1960), I, 736.

2. Lanteri to Msgr. Du Bourg, Sept. 17, 1816, in *Carteggio Lanteri* (Turin, 1976) III, 129.

3. In the letter already cited of Lanteri to Du Bourg of Sept. 17, 1816, it speaks of four priests who had decided to leave for America: Valesano, De Stefanis, Paschetti, Arnaldi. Later, in Louisiana we find another four priests from Piedmont: Giovanni Audisio, Giovanni Battista Carretta, Filippo Borgna and Lorenzo Peyretti, "who were probably recruited by Lanteri" (C. Bona, *La Rinascita missionaria in Italia*, Turin, 1964, 80).

Following the years at Boston and San Vittorino is the novitiate. This is where the religious life properly speaking begins. During an entire year novices dedicate themselves to prayer and study of the spirit and life of Father Lanteri. At the end of this year the novice professes his vows for the first time, receives the religious habit, and enters major studies in theology.

Theological studies are undertaken at the Angelicum in Rome. For four years the seminarians attend classes while living in a local Roman parish, St. Helena's. At this time active participation in the apostolate of the congregation begins. All seminarians take part in teaching catechism, visiting the sick, and serving the poor and young people of the parish. These four years of testing and preparation culminate in the final profession of vows, the diaconate, and ordination to the priesthood.

Formation, however, is a never-ending process. All priests and religious must continue to deepen their spiritual and intellectual lives. For this reason the Oblates encourage continuing specialization in theology and spirituality usually undertaken after some initial years of pastoral experience.

Father Bruno Lanteri used to insist that he was not the true founder of the Oblates of the Virgin Mary. Rather it was his belief that the foundress was our Lady herself. He considered it her work, and in his mind she was the one to guide and motivate its members to complete union with Jesus Christ. Throughout the entire religious life of the Oblates of the Virgin Mary, she plays a fundamental role in coming to know and love her Son. As the Constitutions state:

In fulfillment of their consecrated lives, the Oblates are fully dedicated to the Most Holy Virgin Mary as Mother and Foundress. They cherish filial confidence in her and in her they recognize the very

The Pope and Oblate seminarians after a liturgical ceremony.

An ordination of Oblate priests, San Vittorino, Italy.

model of the Church, as of their own faith and self-dedication; and thus they present her to men.

Through such a generous and heartfelt union with the Mother of God, the Oblates aspire to the perfection to which they are called by following Christ.

For information concerning the Oblates of the Virgin Mary, their form of apostolate, means of formation and spirit, write:

Vocation Director
Our Lady of Grace Seminary
1105 Boylston Street
Boston, Massachusetts 02215
(617-266-5999)

outside of North America contact:
Vocation Director
Istituto N.S. di Fatima
00010 San Vittorino
(Roma) Italy

St. Clement's Eucharistic Shrine and Our Lady of Grace Seminary, Boston, Massachusetts.

Daughters of St. Paul

IN MASSACHUSETTS
  50 St. Paul's Ave. Jamaica Plain, Boston, MA 02130;
    617-522-8911; 617-522-0875;
  172 Tremont Street, Boston, MA 02111; **617-426-5464;**
    617-426-4230
IN NEW YORK
  78 Fort Place, Staten Island, NY 10301; **212-447-5071**
  59 East 43rd Street, New York, NY 10017; **212-986-7580**
  7 State Street, New York, NY 10004; **212-447-5071**
  625 East 187th Street, Bronx, NY 10458; **212-584-0440**
  525 Main Street, Buffalo, NY 14203; **716-847-6044**
IN NEW JERSEY
  Hudson Mall — Route 440 and Communipaw Ave.,
    Jersey City, NJ 07304; **201-433-7740**
IN CONNECTICUT
  202 Fairfield Ave., Bridgeport, CT 06604; **203-335-9913**
IN OHIO
  2105 Ontario St. (at Prospect Ave.), Cleveland, OH 44115; **216-621-9427**
  25 E. Eighth Street, Cincinnati, OH 45202; **513-721-4838**
IN PENNSYLVANIA
  1719 Chestnut Street, Philadelphia, PA 19103; **215-568-2638**
IN FLORIDA
  2700 Biscayne Blvd., Miami, FL 33137; **305-573-1618**
IN LOUISIANA
  4403 Veterans Memorial Blvd., Metairie, LA 70002; **504-887-7631;**
    504-887-0113
  1800 South Acadian Thruway, P.O. Box 2028, Baton Rouge, LA 70821
    504-343-4057; 504-343-3814
IN MISSOURI
  1001 Pine Street (at North 10th), St. Louis, MO 63101; **314-621-0346;**
    314-231-1034
IN ILLINOIS
  172 North Michigan Ave., Chicago, IL 60601; **312-346-4228**
IN TEXAS
  114 Main Plaza, San Antonio, TX 78205; **512-224-8101**
IN CALIFORNIA
  1570 Fifth Avenue, San Diego, CA 92101; **714-232-1442**
  46 Geary Street, San Francisco, CA 94108; **415-781-5180**
IN HAWAII
  1143 Bishop Street, Honolulu, HI 96813; **808-521-2731**
IN ALASKA
  750 West 5th Avenue, Anchorage AK 99501; **907-272-8183**
IN CANADA
  3022 Dufferin Street, Toronto 395, Ontario, Canada
IN ENGLAND
  128, Notting Hill Gate, London W11 3QG, England
  133 Corporation Street, Birmingham B4 6PH, England
  5A-7 Royal Exchange Square, Glasgow G1 3AH, England
  82 Bold Street, Liverpool L1 4HR, England
IN AUSTRALIA
  58 Abbotsford Rd., Homebush, N.S.W., Sydney 2140, Australia